GOSPEL LIGHT

GOSPEL LIGHT

Jesus Stories for Spiritual Consciousness

JOHN SHEA

A Crossroad Book
The Crossroad Publishing Company
New York

This printing: 1999

The Crossroad Publishing Company
370 Lexington Avenue, New York, NY 10017

Copyright © 1998 by John Shea

Printed in the United States of America

Library of Congress Cataloging-in-Publication Data
Shea, John, 1941–
    Gospel light : Jesus stories for spiritual consciousness / John
Shea.
        p.   cm.
    Includes bibliographical references.
    ISBN 0-8245-1709-1 (pbk.)
    1. Spirituality – Catholic Church. 2. Bible. N.T. Gospels –
Devotional literature.   I. Title.
BX2350.65S44   1998
232 – dc21   97-45145
                                                         CIP

To My Mother
Who Knows the Secret

Contents

Preface

Stories as Intermediaries

JALALUDDIN RUMI, a Sufi mystic and poet of the thirteenth cen-
tury, spoke a poem that has been entitled "Story-Water." He
compares a story to bath water. The bath water is heated by fire.
The heated water now carries messages from the fire to the body.
It lets the flame and the skin meet. He remarks:

> Very few can sit down
> in the middle of the fire itself....
> We need intermediaries.*

Stories are intermediaries between "the fire itself" and those who
would be warmed by it.

The "fire itself" is the Spirit that suffuses everything there is.
Spirit is a fire because, in the last analysis, it is passionate love.
Spirit is the flaming bush of Moses that burns but does not burn
out. It is the light John the Evangelist sings about, a light the
darkness cannot overcome. It is what Teilhard de Chardin saw
so clearly at the heart of all matter. When the human race dis-
covers the power of love, he predicted, it will have discovered fire
for the second time. Invisible love is the secret animating power
of the entire world.

However, "very few can sit in the middle of the fire itself."
Most do not touch the divine energy directly. We encounter the
intermediaries. Rumi suggests:

> Study them [stories]
> and enjoy this being washed

---

*Rumi, *One-Handed Basket Weaving,* trans. Coleman Barks Maypop (Athens, Ga.:
Maypop, 1991), 29.

9

> with a secret we sometimes know,
> and then not.

This is a realistic assessment of the mediating ability of stories. Studying them will bring the pleasure of revelation. The secret will be known. But spiritual knowing is often fleeting. What is seen one moment recedes the next moment. The luminous story is suddenly opaque. This swing from knowing to not knowing, from revelation to concealment, is simply how it is. It is essential to the relationship between intermediaries and Spirit. So "enjoy this being washed / with a secret we sometimes know, / and then not."

This is a book about stories as intermediaries of the fire. It takes the advice of Rumi, who was called Maulana, "The Master," and applies it to the stories of Jesus who was also called "The Master." It attempts to study and enjoy Jesus stories and live in the rhythms of knowing and not knowing their spiritual secrets. It delights in what they show and bows to what they hide. I take this attitude to be a high form of respect for the Jesus stories in the gospels.

Part One is foundational. It establishes the context for appreciating the Jesus stories as resources for spiritual consciousness. The first chapter explores the way of spiritual consciousness, how people come to see from a spiritual perspective. It is not merely a matter of stating there is a spiritual force that permeates the human person and the entire universe. The question is: How do we become aware and stay aware of this Spirit? How do we feel the heat of the fire? The ancient directive is: go within to go without. Spiritual consciousness is a way of seeing the world from the soul space, and we enter the soul space by an interior journey. This soul-seeing generates wisdom. It helps us appreciate every aspect of life from a spiritual perspective. This wisdom, in turn, spurs us to act. Once within, we go without. Spirit fills and flows. We join its energy. Fire — even through a story intermediary — burns those who touch it.

The second chapter of Part One suggests a way to appropriate Jesus stories. In Luke's story, traditionally called "The Road to Emmaus," the two travelers say, "Did not our hearts burn within us as he spoke to us on the way and opened up for us the scriptures?"

In the biblical tradition scripture stories have been successful intermediaries. They have been consulted "on the way" and they have burned many hearts. How can this tradition continue? How today can we relate to the Jesus stories so they accompany us "on the way" and communicate to us the fire? Too often they are only cold coals. I retrace my own path of telling and meditating on Jesus stories in the hope of finding a useful approach. I find there are clues in my reluctance to treat Jesus stories as "tales to be performed," in my attempts to make Jesus stories my own, and in my ongoing efforts to offer to others these burning tales.

Part Two has six chapters. Each chapter unfolds a specific Jesus story from one of the four gospels. Individually and collectively they are explorations of the way of spiritual consciousness that was mapped out in chapter 1. They chart the perils and promises of going within to go without. "Going within to go without" sounds like a bland journey. However, when Jesus stories are the intermediaries for this spiritual process, the fire is close. We are not sitting in the fire itself, but we know it has been cast upon the earth.

I have gathered the Jesus stories in a spiritual sequence suggested by the parables of the treasure in the field and the pearl of great price. The parallel plots are: a man *finds* a treasure in a field or a pearl of great price, he goes with joy and *sells* all he has, and he *buys* the field or pearl. The unfolding spiritual dynamic is financially imaged as finding, selling, and buying.

Finding connects with the spiritual themes of awakening and revelation. We suddenly become aware of a dimension of ourselves and the universe we had not previously seen. In particular, we begin to sense that we are more than our roles, our responsibilities, our bodily appetites, and our mental functionings. We uncover a selfhood that the Spanish poet Antonio Machado suggested was a core truth of Christ:

> He [Christ] spoke another truth:
> Find the you that is not yours
> and never can be.*

---

*Antonio Machado, *Selected Poems* (Cambridge, Mass.: Harvard University Press, 1982), 187.

Our deepest identity (*the you*) does not belong to us (*that is not yours*), and we should not strive to possess it (*and never can be*). Paul said it simply, "You are not your own." The Jesus stories that explore this treasure in the field and this pearl of great price are "The Sound of the Wind" (the Nicodemus story from John 2:23–3:21) and "The Voice from the Sky and the Struggles of the Earth" (the baptism, genealogy, temptations, and homecoming from Luke 3:21–4:30).

Selling connects with the spiritual themes of detachment, letting go and dying. In order to enter more deeply into the spiritual identity of the "you that is not yours and never will be," we need to let go of our attachments to wounds, mistakes, and failures. Also we have to allow other people to cut the knot they have tied to their pain. Stripping away rigid accretions and letting go of what makes us blind and deaf are essential to spiritual development. In the gospels this is the emphasis on forgiveness of sins, a process of dying to the many false selves we have become enslaved to. The two Jesus stories that explore these dynamics are "The Traveling Pallet" (the paralyzed man from Mark 2:1–12) and "The Truth of Twice" (the woman taken in adultery from John 8:1–11).

Buying connects with the spiritual themes of risk and commitment. It focuses on a complete "buy-in," a whole-hearted attempt at life in the Spirit. In the gospels this means entering into the processes of receiving and giving. Matthew sums it up in four words. "Freely receiving, freely giving" (Matt. 10:8). Buying symbolizes a participation in the endless rhythms of receiving Spirit from the Divine Source at every moment and giving it into the world at every moment. This is as close to the fire as Christians get without sitting in it. The stories that explore this intimate interaction between receiving and giving are "The Secret of the Towel" (the footwashing episode from John 13:1–17) and "The Road Less Traveled Is the Road Back" (the Last Supper, the road to Emmaus, and the Gethsemane story from Luke 22:14, 19–20; 24:13–35; 22:39–53).

Each gospel story is laid out line by line with interpretations and explorations spliced in between. This is the classic commentary style, but this is not a classic commentary. The interpretations presuppose but do not mimic the work of biblical scholars. For the most part they bypass philology, history, and the marshaling of conflicting and concurring opinions. What happens between the lines is the work of a storyteller and spiritual teacher. Together we will study the characters, play with the plots, and lure into the open the hidden spiritual dynamics. In this way the intermediary nature of the story will emerge and we will be warmed by the fire.

Stories that communicate fire provoke reflection. So after each Jesus story there are two reflections. These are thoughts and vignettes the Jesus story has brought to mind and heart. These ponderings attempt to weave the spiritual wisdom of the Jesus stories into the fabric of contemporary life. Or, if this is too ambitious, at least they will select an image or insight and develop it beyond the boundaries of the story.

Written on the wall at Delphi was the inscription "Invoked or not, God is present." Spiritual consciousness is the birthright of all people. They may or may not invoke God, but Spirit is present. The universal presence of Spirit coupled with the growing contemporary quest for Spirit is the theological and cultural context of this book. Although this book uses the Jesus stories as the particular way into the life of the Spirit, it is not meant "For Christians Only." It is meant for all people who are searching for deeper spiritual realizations. What Jesus said about himself to the skeptical Pilate holds true for all the Jesus stories. "For this I was born and for this I have come into the world, to bear witness to the truth. Everyone who is of the truth hears my voice" (John 18:37). The stories reveal truths to all those who seek after truth. They bring the fire close. If we are attentive, we can see by its light, be warmed by its heat, and enjoy the secret "we sometimes know, then not."

Part 1

SPIRITUAL CONSCIOUSNESS AND STORYTELLING

Chapter 1

The Way of Spiritual Consciousness
GOING WITHIN TO GO WITHOUT

E VERY NIGHT, when my father came home from work, he would do the same thing. I was six, and every night I watched him.

We lived on the second floor of a two-flat. I could hear him coming up the stairs before I could see him. When he came through the door, I was there. He would pat me on my crew cut and take off his hat and plop it on my head. It would slide forward over my eyes and sideways over my ears. All this was done while he was walking, while he was making his way toward the bedroom, while I was following, pushing the hat back to see.

My father was a policeman. He carried a gun in a holster at his hip. It was not slung low like the cowboy gunslingers in the serials I saw at the West End Theater on Saturday mornings. It rode waist high. Once, as we were walking toward the bedroom, I asked him if he could draw fast enough with the gun that high.

"It's not like that," he said.

On the top shelf of the closet in my mother and father's bedroom was a wooden safe. My father had it made to size, and it was a snug fit, perfect height and perfect depth. On the shelf next to the safe was a key. With his back to me, my father would open the closet door, take the key off the shelf, and open the safe. Then he would take off his belt and holster and take the gun out of the holster. The holster and belt would be rolled up and stuffed way back in the safe. Then he would open the cylinder of the gun. The bullets would slide out into his free hand. He would put the bullets in a dish that was inside the safe. I could hear them clinking as they rolled and settled into place. Then he would put the gun into the safe, lock it, and put the key on the shelf. This is what he would do every night when he came home — as I watched.

One night, after he had put the bullets in the dish, he turned and walked over to me. He was holding the gun by the barrel. Without saying anything, he offered me the handle. I took it. Its heaviness surprised me. My arm fell to my side. I quickly heaved my arm up. It was all I do to hold it upright. My father took it out of my hand, opened the cylinder, and rolled it.

"This is where the bullets go," he said. "When you pull the trigger, the chambers move."

He paused.

"Do you want to play with it?" he finally said.

I nodded.

He gave me the gun. "Don't pull the trigger."

I went to the window and pointed the gun at the two-flat next door.

I looked at my father. He was watching me, but he said nothing.

I went over to the bed, hid behind it, then popped up and aimed.

My father said nothing.

I put the gun in my pocket and jerked it out. Fastdraw.

My father said nothing.

I put the gun in my belt and pulled it out. Fasterdraw.

My father said nothing.

I lay on the floor and took aim. Gunshot sounds came out of my mouth.

My father said, "Are you done?"

I nodded and handed him the gun. He turned and went to the safe. As he was locking the gun away, with his back to me, he said, "There — now you don't have to be figuring out how to get it all the time."

His words stunned me. It was not because they were critical or unkind. They were not. In fact, they were said in a completely matter-of-fact voice. There was no judgment in what he said. There was something far more shocking than judgment. There was truth. He was right. I *was* figuring out how to get it. But until he said it, I didn't know that was what I was doing. I did not know my watching was really a spying. I was "casing" the closet for a future raid, but I didn't know it. He knew me before I knew myself, and he gently showed me to myself.

As far as I can remember that was the first time I realized there was more going on in me than I knew. Of course, it was not the last time. Over the years I have been invited by certain events and strong-armed by others into "going inside." I was often reluctant to undertake this inner scrutiny. The entertainments in the outer world always seemed more attractive. However, when I have managed to sustain an inner journey, there has always been a payoff. Most often the payoff has been painful. Knowing the hidden holdings of the mind is usually a blow to any scrubbed-up persona, any idealized self-image. But the pain is not as debilitating as the revelation is intriguing. Tearing the veil and seeing what has been cloaked is a temptation few can resist. This is part of what Jung meant when he said the development takes places not by "entertaining figures of light, but by making the darkness visible."

In workshops it is sometimes suggested that people write their religious autobiography. I suppose I could start mine with awesome memories of gothic churches with their vaulted ceilings, dark interiors, flickering lights, and the lingering smell of incense. Or perhaps I could recount the first time my mother taught me to pray before sleeping. Or, going back to personally unconscious moments, baptism obviously would be a theologically correct choice, and who could argue with birth as a beginning? These experiences, among others, are candidates for catapulting me into a sense of religion and faith. However, when I think of my spiritual development, I gravitate to the gun and the sudden revelation of an interior landscape. It was my first turn from the outer world, my first glance, however fleeting, into the inner labyrinth. Most importantly, it was my first taste of spiritual freedom.

Once I recognized my gun fantasy, I was free to say no or yes to its insistent demands. That is one of the benefits of making the unconscious conscious. We now no longer relate *from* the secret conditionings of the mind; we relate *to* them. This diminishes their power to control our responses. This ability to modify hidden conditionings usually takes a long time and a lot of practice. It becomes a spiritual ascesis, a discipline of recognition, a training of consciousness. We are no longer owned by our buried compulsions. When we have knowledge of what we carry, we carry it more lightly. That is the sweet taste of spiritual freedom, and, whatever else it is, it is addictive.

Experiences like these can be a beginning. They open us to deeper levels. They place our feet on an interior path that eventually leads consciousness to the soul space where it glimpses the infinity of Spirit. However, for this to happen there has to be encouragement and guidance. It is here, I believe, that the spiritual traditions of the world enter into the lives of spiritual seekers. Spiritual traditions know about breakthrough moments, times when consciousness shifts and the hidden is revealed. In fact, they know more about them than those who experience them. Spiritual traditions pick up the little we know and put it in the context of all they know. In this way they assure the spiritually sensitive they are not alone. What they have experienced is a genuine human potential that is able to be cultivated. The breakthrough occurs in individual experience; the nurture comes from spiritual traditions.

Spiritual traditions provide visions, maps, and guides — in that order. First, they function as resources for spiritual seekers by providing descriptions of what they will find. These are tales of treasure, assurances that something awaits us that is the fulfillment of every human striving. Of course, the treasure is talked about in ways that are enticingly vague. There is plenty of room for surprise. Secondly, the spiritual traditions lay out maps that show the way to the treasure. Of course, the maps are not the territory. If we attempt to follow the maps, we will find much more than is sketched. We will seldom find less. Thirdly, there are guides. Women and men have walked this way and they are willing to take us by the hand. Of course, at some point they will let go of our hand. This is our journey, and we must realize the truths of the Spirit for ourselves. In the visions, maps, and guides there is encouragement and direction but not complete disclosure. The secret is talked about but it is not given away. Spiritual traditions provide all the resources that are needed. However, they leave the shock of discovery to us.

But before maps and guides, there are tales of treasure, enticements to begin, pictures that create fire in the mind, possibilities so tied to human nature that to ignore their lure is to miss something essential.

Hidden Treasure

The spiritual tradition that encourages "going within" can be traced to the ancient, enigmatic imperative "Know thyself." Plotinus elaborated on this directive. "We must close our eyes and invoke a new manner of seeing, a wakefulness that is the birthright of us all, though few put it to use." This suggests we are out of touch with who we are. The journey of self-knowledge is an adventure into the unknown. "Going within" will be a movement from ignorance to wisdom. In the classic metaphors of spiritual teachings we will move from being asleep to being awake, from being lost to being found, from death to life, from blindness to sight, from deafness to hearing. All these metaphors suggest treasure, a fuller and more abundant life. However, this treasure is close. We are strange pilgrims, journeying to become who we really are.

I once gave a talk on spirituality that tried to point out that we may be more than we know. We may have a divine-human birthright, although "few put it to use." Someone from the audience asked for clarification. "Is this what you were *trying* to say? I was a teacher for many years," he explained. "Every Christmas most of the students would give me a token gift. After a while you didn't have to be a fortune teller to guess what the gifts would be. Especially if it came in a long flat box. It was a handkerchief. It got to a point where I never opened those flat boxes. I just stacked them in my closet. Whenever I needed a handkerchief, I opened one up. One day I opened a box and inside was an antique pocket watch. All this time I had an antique pocket watch, and I didn't know it. Is that what you were trying to say?"

"Not only is that what I was trying to say," I replied. "That says it better than I said it."

It also connects with other images of the spiritual life that attempt to convey a similar insight. We have a vintage wine cellar, and we rarely drink from it. We have an interior castle, and we seldom visit it. There is a treasure buried in our field, and we do not know how to unearth it. Meister Eckhart recalled that Abraham dug wells of living water. An enemy came and threw dirt into those wells. Although the dirt kept the wells from springing forth, the gushing water was still there. A final image, and a favorite of writers on the spiritual life, is the beclouded sun. The sun constantly shines. Sometimes clouds cover it, and we cannot see it. Even though we cannot see it, the sun does not stop shining. These images attempt to drive home the same insight. There is more to who we are than we know. There is a distinction between reality and our awareness of it. A dimension of our reality is an antique watch, a wine cellar, an interior castle, a buried treasure, a gushing well, a shining sun. There is something rare, valuable, royal, refreshing, and radiant about us. However, we may not realize or appreciate ourselves in this way.

Teaching-stories from diverse spiritual traditions drive home the same point. There is the classic story of the poor man who dreams of treasure in a another city. He travels to that city to unearth the treasure. But before he can get to it, he meets a man who tells him he is going on a similar quest. His destination is a poor man's shabby house where a treasure is hidden behind the bricks of the fireplace. The poor man realizes the house of this man's dreams is his own. He quickly returns home to find the treasure that was always there.

A similar tale starts with a man who is disgruntled with his wife, children, and neighbors. They are disrespectful, disobedient, and cantankerous. He prays to God for relief. God tells him to prepare to journey to a far land where he will arrange the ideal wife, children, and neighbors. The man begins his journey. On his first night he is deep in the woods. He is afraid he will become disoriented in his sleep and lose his way. So he places his shoes in the direction he wishes to go. In the morning the shoes will tell him which way to travel.

However, while he is asleep, an angel comes and turns the shoes around. So the next day he is returning to his old village, only he does not know it. As he draws near, he is surprised to find a wife that looks like his own wife, children who look like his own children, neighbors who look like his old neighbors. He thinks God has arranged this similarity to comfort him. He has a new heart within him, one that knows God loves him. Correspondingly, his wife, children, and neighbors now treat him lovingly, obediently, and friendly. To find love, respect, and companionship he did not have to travel far. He had to go within to what was near, but far from his consciousness. A new inner sense of himself generated a new outer world. Once again, the treasure was close but unrecognized.

There is another tale about hidden treasure, a tale that is more a joke than a story. This joke has been around a long time. It has even found its way into print and been commented on by people interested in spirituality. Some have suggested that it is a brand of esoteric Christianity. It works on two levels, the conventional surface and the hidden depth. If you "get" both levels, the initial laugh will be followed by a longer, more enduring smile — the smile that accompanies the seeing of a spiritual truth.

Jesus and Moses were playing golf. They came to a long par three — 220 yards with a 200-yard carry over water. Jesus was first up. He was addressing the ball when Moses asked, "What are you using?"

"A five iron," Jesus replied.

"A five iron?" Moses was incredulous. "You can't carry the water with a five iron. You need more club."

"Tiger Woods hits a five iron," Jesus replied. (This joke has been updated. I have heard it with both Arnold Palmer and Jack Nicklaus in this featured role.)

Jesus swung and hit a long arching five that, alas, carried only 165 yards. It splashed in the pond.

"I'll get it," Moses said.

Moses walked down to the water, which obediently parted before him. He strode out, like Charlton Heston, on dry ground to Jesus' ball, picked it up, and walked back to the tee — the water filling in neatly behind him.

Jesus took the ball from Moses, teed up, and was ready to hit.

"What club are you using?" Moses asked.

"A five iron," Jesus replied.

"A five iron?" Moses was incredulous a second time. "You can't carry the water with a five iron. You need more club."

"Tiger Woods hits a five iron," Jesus said.

Jesus hit a long arching five that carried about 180 yards before it splashed into the pond.

"Don't bother," said Jesus, preempting Moses' offer. "I'll get it."

Jesus strode down to the pond and calmly walked out on the water in search of his ball.

Just then the foursome behind Jesus and Moses arrived at the tee. They saw Jesus walking on the water.

They said to Moses, "Who does that guy think he is — Jesus Christ?"

"He is Jesus Christ," Moses replied. "But he thinks he's Tiger Woods."

The background of this joke is a popular way we have of "putting people in their place." When they "show off" or try something a little beyond their powers and abilities, we remind them that they are a little less than they think they are. "Who do you think you are — Jesus Christ?" is a roundabout religious way of saying "get off it." When people who think they can walk on air are brought thumpingly back to earth, it is always good for a laugh and, most of the time, a needed spiritual corrective. Spiritual pretensions are fun to deflate. When people are on a spiritual path and the path is all too obviously an ego trip, "Who do you think you are, Jesus Christ?" is the voice of sanity.

However, this familiar "get back in place" message is the setup for the joke, not the punch line. The punch line is an unexpected reversal. It is not a case of someone who is lesser parading himself as greater and, therefore, in need of an earthly reminder. It is someone who is greater insisting on being lesser and, therefore, in need of a heavenly reminder. Who he thinks he is is less than who he really is. It is a case of mistaken identity. "He is Jesus Christ, but he thinks he's Tiger Woods."

Although this joke may tell us nothing about Jesus of Nazareth who is the Christ, it might tell us a great deal about ourselves. Most people are in touch with the physical, psychological, and social dimensions of themselves. In fact, there is a tendency to identify with these real but limited aspects. If we have a full head of hair, we tend to confer on it a "this is me" quality and designate ourselves as "he of the radiant locks." Or if we manage an "A" in economics, we quickly collapse ourselves into this academic glory and become "she of the great intellect." Or if we work as a chief operating officer in a marketing firm, one day we may find our attachment to this position so complete, we say to ourselves and others as if nothing more could be said, "I am a COO." Of if we have had a powerful experience of being abandoned by someone we love, we may so internalize that single, transitory experience that we think of ourselves as "the rejected one." Or if we are successful at ingratiating ourselves with other people, we may come to know ourselves as "the charmer." At any given moment we are tempted to equate our identity with a physical quality, a mental attribute, a social role, a significant experience, or a personality trait. We do not have to be reminded that human complexity entails all these things, these "Tiger Woods" aspects of ourselves. We are in constant interaction with them.

However, there is another aspect of the human condition that often goes unnoticed. We are also a spiritual reality. Spiritual teachers talk about this dimension in many different ways. Some call it "essence" or "heart" or "soul" or "the true self." Christian traditions express this truth as being a son or daughter of God or being made in the image of God. Since this truth is known through Jesus Christ, a further designation is made. Christians are sons and daughters in the Son or images of the Image (Jesus Christ) of God. Indebtedness and connectedness to Jesus Christ are an essential part of Christian identity. In this sense the deepest truth about Christians is they are Jesus Christ, even if at times they fall to lesser identifications and think they are Tiger Woods. With apologies to a great young golfer, this is the esoteric interpretation of the joke.

These images and stories resonate with a witty warning from the *Gospel of Thomas*.

> Jesus said,
> "If those who lead you say to you,
> 'See, the kingdom is in the sky,'
> then the birds of the sky will precede you.
>
> If they say to you,
> 'It is in the sea,'
> then the fish of the sea will precede you.
>
> But the kingdom is within you
> and it is without you.
>
> If you will know yourselves,
> then you will be known and you will know
> that you are sons and daughters of the Living One.
>
> But if you do not know yourselves,
> then you are in poverty and you are poverty."

The talk of treasure is to lure us out of poverty and into the knowledge that we are daughters and sons of the Living One. Maps to this interior wealth are available.

A Map of the Outer World

The first direction in knowing yourself is to go within. This direction is often expanded by adding the adjective, "deep." Go deep within. This depth descent hopes to find a grounding, a foundation that supports the whole enterprise of the human person. Another addition to "go within" is "to your spiritual center." This image of center suggests what will ultimately be found will radiate throughout everything else. The center identifies something that everything else participates in. Therefore, the path of self-knowledge is "to go deep within to the spiritual center."

However, going within is not the easiest direction for consciousness to take. Consciousness is naturally attracted to the outer world. The five senses open us to that world. Its sights, sounds, touches, tastes, and smells keep us occupied and entertained. I wake in the morning to the radio alarm that tells me the weather and traffic. I move from the dream consciousness of interiority to the waking consciousness of exteriority. If I am going to get through to Friday, my consciousness will have to stay in this outer world. I will have to negotiate razor blades, stoplights, employer innuendoes, expiration dates on milk cartons, unmatching ties, deadlines, and sidewalks where dogs have preceded me. There is more than enough to do in the outer world before sleep returns.

Also the outer world is a place of action. It is where things are happening and, as the experience-glutton in us all says, "I don't want to miss anything." There is a strong cultural bias toward immersion in the activity-driven outer world. Introspection is suspect. Any suggestion that inner work might be appropriate has to contend with the mental tape that says it is a waste of time. "I'll never get anything done. I don't want to become a navel gazer." I am always struck by the fact we often fear what we have the least chance of becoming. I once did a storytelling session with a group of college professors. When I finished, the first response was, "Don't you fear this storytelling approach will lead to irrationalism?" Everyone present had a Ph.D. Irrationalism could not have broken into that room with an Uzi. In the same way, the average active American is not threatened by going within. Quietism has no chance of sweeping the country. The fear that a little meditation will make you a monk is greatly exaggerated.

The more persuasive reason we hesitate to move within is because we are addicted to without. At least that is the discernment of many spiritual teachers. We are caught in chronic busyness and feel good about ourselves only when we are doing something. It is this preexisting condition that makes people laugh when they first hear the unconventional advice attributed to the Buddha, "Don't just do something. Stand there." This aphorism is deepened by the reflection of a Tibetan Buddhist text: "Freedom is not the opposite of determinism, but of compulsion, of having to act." If the outer world of action is the only place you can be, it is not the place you should be all the time.

The entrapments of the outer world and the disabilities it produces are favorite themes of spiritual teaching-stories. A major symbol in many of these stories is clothing. Garments are what people first see, and so they represent the exterior covering of the body, mind, and soul. They are the outer edge, the surface of a much deeper reality. However, we may never appreciate this deeper reality because of our tendency to become trapped by either the elegance or disarray of the clothes. We ourselves want fine clothes, and we admire the fine clothes of others. Spiritual teachers use this simple human trait to show how consciousness gets caught in externals.

There is a story from the Jewish tradition about Elijah, who is not only the prophet of biblical legend but also a bit of a trickster and magician. He is walking through a town when he hears the sounds of a party coming from a very large and beautiful house. He swirls around and instantly he is clothed in the rags of a beggar. He knocks on the door. The host answers, takes one look at Elijah's miserable clothing, and slams the door in his face. Elijah swirls around a second time and is instantly clothed in the fine garments of a gentleman. He knocks on the door. The host answers, takes one look at his splendid attire, and ushers him in.

At the feast there is a long table of food. Elijah goes to it immediately and begins stuffing food into his pockets. The guests step back to watch this strange sight. Then he pushes more food inside his shirt and pours wine over his shoulders and down the front of his fine attire. The host is irritated and asks Elijah what he thinks he is doing. Elijah replies, "I came to your door dressed in rags and you did not invite me in. Then I came to your door — the same person — dressed in fine garments and you welcomed me to your feast. I could only conclude that it was not me that you invited but my clothes. So I fed them with your food and drink." The story says that the people were ashamed. They looked down. When they looked up, Elijah was gone.

A second story concerns a man who goes to a tailor to buy a suit of clothes. He tries it on in front of the mirror and notices the suit coat is a little uneven at the bottom. "It needs a hand adjustment," the tailor suggests. "Just pull it down with your hand." The man does this, looks in the mirror and notices that the lapel has popped up. He is told it needs a "chin adjustment." So he puts his chin on the popped-up lapel to keep it down. Finally, the pants are too tight in the crotch and have to be pulled down by a hand adjustment. Although he is bent over and crippled by the many "alterations," he buys the suit. The next day he is walking through the park with his new suit. He passes two old men sitting on a bench. The first comments on how crippled the poor man is. The second one agrees and adds, "Yes...but I wonder where he got such a nice suit."

There is a considerable amount of "bite" in these two stories. They cannot see Elijah because they cannot get past his clothing. It is not a story of Elijah disguising himself but of people blinding themselves. Their judgments are no deeper than clothes. "What did you go out into the desert to see? A man dressed in fine garments?" (Luke 7:24). Also we twist ourselves out of shape so we will look good in the mirror. Our inner reality is ignored. We give ourselves completely over to appearance. The outer world is all that matters. We do not see the crippling cost to the deeper dimensions of ourselves. These are some of the excesses that occur when consciousness is totally outer-directed.

Direct spiritual teaching emphasizes similar problems. The Dhammapada attacks the seductive powers of externals:

> What is the use of plaited hair, O fool? What of the raiment of goatskins? Within thee there is ravening, but outside thou makest clean. The one who wears dirty raiments, who is emaciated and covered with veins, who meditates alone in the forest, that one I call indeed a Brahmana.

Even religious activity which is meant to bring consciousness to deeper interior levels gets caught parading for the outer world. Jesus cautions that this could happen to prayer.

> When you pray, you must not be like the hypocrites. They
> love to stand and pray in the synagogues and at the street
> corners so they may be seen by people.... But when you
> pray, go into your room and shut the door and pray to your
> Father who is in secret; and your Father who sees in secret
> will reward you. (Matt. 6:5–6)

A similar warning is given for almsgiving and fasting. The message is clear. When the outer world monopolizes attention, the inner world is neglected. This inner world is the hidden place of communion with the divine. If we do not visit it, the relationship to God withers.

Therefore, going within is both important and resisted, promising and forbidding. There are two traditional strategies that address this ambivalence. First, going within is helped by "going away." This going away is a quest after solitude. It may be a retreat center in Vermont, an isolated stretch of beach in Washington, a church or synagogue or mosque that is open during the week, a park, or even a room in your house with a door that closes. In these places the pressing in of the outer world may lessen. When we close down the outer world, the inner world will begin to open. This traditional strategy, and it is only a strategy, has been called the "turtle pulls in its feet." We are pulling consciousness within, and it helps if we are in a place where the outer world is not furiously pulling consciousness outside.

Second, the inducement to go within can be supported by the promise to return. Going within is not about staying within. It is about discovering something that will allow a much different way of being without. When consciousness returns to the outer world, it will bring with it a new perspective. This new perspective will increase our pleasure and creativity in the outer world. We will see and hear differently. An order will be brought to the chaos, a direction to the randomness, a sense of peace to the franticness. Going within is not a path of escape but a path of reengagement. Of course, what is not mentioned, what is part of the secret of the hidden treasure, is that we do not return to the outer world as an outer world. We return to the outer world as a spiritually grounded world.

A Map of the Inner World: The Body

When consciousness goes within, it immediately sets up a relationship with the body. Our attention to our body is usually confined to times when it makes a disturbance. When we stub our toe or our stomach growls or we get something caught in our eye or our bowels won't cooperate or our back stiffens or we bite our tongue, our attention goes into our body. Consciousness follows clamoring. Otherwise, in an ancient image, the body is just the horse we ride or, in a modern image, it is the car we drive.

But once consciousness is within, it can explore the body when it is relatively calm. This non-judgmental body scan is usually a revelation. We discover valleys and mountains, deserts stretches and lush gardens, night storms and windless days. I believe it was James Joyce who once wrote, "Mr. Duffy lived a short distance from his body." When consciousness goes within, that distance can be bridged. The first inner territory of the spiritual journey is the body.

However, this first step is often stepped over. Spiritual traditions have the reputation of alienating people from their bodies. Their primary concern was the higher reaches of the soul that opened into the divine. The lower reaches of the soul that informed the body were noted, but they were not as thoroughly charted. As consciousness went deeper and uncovered more profound dimensions of the self, there was the temptation to devalue the body. More integrated spiritual teachers resisted that temptation. They stressed that deeper consciousness provided an opportunity for a more healing relationship to the body. Yet the rhetoric of much teaching gave the opposite impression. "Leave behind the things of earth and seek the things of heaven.... As garments are the covering of the body, the body is the covering of the soul." In these mistaken evaluations the earth is abandoned and the body is treated as part of the outer world.

However, the real inner journey does not use a scalpel. It is not a matter of stripping away the lower and what some consider the non-essential dimensions of the human. As consciousness deepens, it participates in a dynamic of transcendence and acceptance, not transcendence and rejection. Nothing is lost or abandoned or gone beyond. Consciousness includes where it has been in where it it going. The body nests within the mind, the mind nests within the soul, and the soul nests within Spirit. We are a differentiated whole, and, as the Bible commands, no one should split asunder what God has joined. The question is how to integrate the multidimensional reality of the human person.

Today the relationship of consciousness to the body is an area of increasing exploration. Can we send loving energies into certain parts of our bodies? Does meditation help high blood pressure? Can consciousness reclaim alienated physical parts of ourselves and reintegrate them into the whole of who we are? Whatever the answers to these questions are, the first territory consciousness travels when it goes within is our physical make-up. We learn to explore and set up a relationship with aspects of our bodies and with our bodies as a whole. This ability to relate to our bodies often releases the healing powers of the deeper regions of ourselves.

In the autobiographical essay "Beauty: When the Other Dancer Is the Self" Alice Walker tells of her ongoing relationship with her wounded eye.* As a small girl she was hit in the eye with a bee-bee and lost her sight. As she grew older, this unseeing eye became a major player in her life, entering into her relationships and her work. Her family convinces her to get it "fixed." This means to have the scar removed. A plastic surgeon does the job. However, what is left is a small bluish indentation. The ugly yellowish-white scar is gone. Now there is a blue crater in the eye of a black woman.

She has a baby and she worries what the child will think when she sees her mother's eyes are different from other people's. Her child is three, and every day she watches a program called "Big Blue Marble." It begins with a picture of the earth as it appears

---

*Alice Walker, *In Search of Our Mother's Gardens* (New York: Harcourt Brace, 1983).

from the moon. It is bluish and a little battered looking. One day when Alice is putting Rebecca down for her nap, the child focuses on her eye. "Something inside me cringes, gets ready to try to protect myself. All children are cruel about physical differences, I know that from experience, and that they don't mean to be is another matter. I assume Rebecca will be the same."

But she is not. She stares at her mother's eye and then says very seriously, "Mommy, there's a world in your eye.... Mommy, where did you get that world in your eye?" This so jolts Alice Walker that she runs to the washroom laughing and crying. She looks at her eye in the mirror and realizes the truth of what her child said. There was a world in her eye. "And I saw that it was possible to love it: that in fact for all it had taught me of shame and anger and inner vision, I *did* love it." That night she has a dream that she is dancing to a Stevie Wonder song. Suddenly another dancer joins her. They dance and kiss and hold each other through the night. "The other dancer has obviously come through all right, as I have done. She is beautiful, whole and free. And she is also me."

A second tale of consciousness setting up a new relationship to the body comes from Joan Didion.* In her autobiographical essay "In Bed" she unfolds her ongoing relationship to her migraine headaches. She has taken up any number of attitudes toward the migraine. She has denied it, fought it, and tried to understand it. But now she thinks she is "wise in its ways":

> I no longer fight it. I lie down and let it happen. At first every small apprehension is magnified, every anxiety a pounding terror. Then the pain comes, and I concentrate only on that. Right there is the usefulness of migraine, there in that imposed yoga, the concentration on the pain. For when the pain recedes, ten or twelve hours later, everything goes with it, all the hidden resentments, all the vain anxieties. The migraine has acted as a circuit breaker, and the fuses have emerged intact. There is a pleasant convalescent euphoria. I open the windows and feel the air, eat gratefully, sleep well. I

---

*Joan Didion, *The White Album* (New York: Simon and Schuster, 1979).

notice the particular nature of a flower in a glass on the stair landing. I count my blessings.

I once read an essay that suggested we learn to smile at our internal organs. I smiled — but not at my internal organs. Besides, my liver is shy and it would blush. But when consciousness goes within, it becomes aware of the body and the multitude of attitudes — from ignoring to indifference to anxiety to pity to love — it has toward the heart or genitals or lungs or legs. Alice Walker and Joan Didion managed to accept a wounded eye and a pounding head. In order to do this, they had to be more than the wounded eye and pounding head. Yet this more did not deny their bodies, even their hurting bodies, but included them along the inner path of transcendence.

A Map of the Inner World: The Mind

As consciousness deepens, it goes beyond the relationship to the body. The mind begins to come into view, and another complex relationship begins to be formed. This is what happened to me when my father said, "There — now you don't have to be figuring out how to get it all the time." I saw the contents of my mind. It was only a peek. But it was enough. I believe the first glimpse of the dynamics of the mind is often through the mirrors others hold up to us. People show us to ourselves, and we are stunned to find out they are right. We are often the last to know. This is because we are so closely identified with our thoughts that we cannot step back and see them. Others help us in this process of observation and so encourage us along the path of mind transcendence. Once we know we are a little bit more than one specific thought, we suspect we are a little bit more than all thoughts. We begin to watch the mind. It is quite a show, an inner cinema. Hollywood would be envious.

My relationship with my mind took a dramatic leap forward when I was fourteen. It was then I started meditating. My spiritual director suggested that I arrive at church a half hour before Mass and meditate. Weekday Mass was at 6:30. When the janitor opened the door at 6:00, I was there. So were about forty older women dressed in black. Widows. I knelt down in a pew and opened my *Meditation Mechanics* book (I kid you not!). But the widows were whispering to one another and clanging coins down the metal chute of the vigil light stand. There was too much noise, even in church, to meditate. Distractions — as the lingo of the day had it — were everywhere.

I told my spiritual director the problem. He suggested I go to church at a time when it was relatively empty. I found myself in the church at 7:30 at night with my basketball next to me in the pew. I had a game at eight. I was alone. The church was completely empty. I opened my meditation book and settled in to meditate. For comfort I sloughed my rear end down onto the pew. Suddenly I heard a voice. "Kneel up straight." It was my grandmother. What was she doing here? More to the point, where was she? She was in my mind. And she was not alone. Over the next couple of months I discovered the noise in the outer world was nothing compared to the noise in the inner world. My mind was running without my permission. Later in life when I came upon the phrase "Thoughts think themselves," I immediately nodded in agreement. When I heard the Buddhist phrase "The mind is a drunken monkey," I knew what zoo that monkey lived in.

One facet of relating to the mind is learning its mechanistic moves. Things happen and the mind moves. Things don't happen and the mind moves. It has a life of its own. As we relate to it, we can shape that life to the larger purposes of who we are. If this relationship is not developed, the mind exercises its considerable power in darkness. The mind, it is said, makes a good servant but a poor master. Turning it into a servant certainly requires discipline. But on a deeper level, it is only the flow of love from the deeper source of the soul that will calm it.

Sebastian Moore, a teacher and theologian, tells about an experience of discovering and relating to his mind.* He was teaching a class that he thought was going very well. One day a fellow teacher told him that he had overheard some of his students

---

*Sebastian Moore, *The Crucified Jesus Is No Stranger* (New York: Seabury Press, 1977).

saying that they hadn't a clue about what was going on. This information flattened Moore. He went back to his room, "dead, destroyed, angry."

However, after a while, he began to ask what was going on here. Slowly he came to realize that it was not the information he had received that was causing him pain. It was the way he was processing the information. He was the victim of a euphoria tape in his mind. This tape programmed him to have "everything going splendidly or else I will resign." But this is not the way of actual life. The real situation is always that this student has understood, and that one has not, and that other one thinks she has but has understood something else. However, the mental tape will have none of this nuance, none of this way-of-things. The conditioning of his mind was blocking his entry into the give-and-take of real life.

Once we understand that the mind enters into every experience, we have an alternate path for reflection. We can continue to analyze our situations from their visible, exterior dynamics. This is the conventional and socially acceptable way of proceeding. But we can also ask how the mind is contributing to the total experience. What is it adding or omitting to what is happening? Many experiences cannot be changed in their outer world dynamics, but they can be changed in their inner world interpretation. In order for this powerful human potential to be developed, it is not enough to have a mind. We must have a relationship to our mind.

Spiritual teachers often guide their disciples along this inner path of freedom and change. They begin by pointing out a facet of mental activity that is often not noticed. It is right there, "hidden in plain sight," or "right above your nose," so to speak. Making the obvious visible is an important moment in spiritual development. The Sufi say about Jesus, "He stands by the river selling river water." He does not supply missing information. Spiritual development is a gradual opening of consciousness to include more and more of what is present. Spiritual wisdom is seeing more of what is and seeing everything there is from the point of view of spirit. The guide merely says, "Notice this. Is it not there?"

Notice that the flip side of discovering the holdings of the mind is the recognition of who is doing the discovering. The moment I saw the holding of my mind — the moment my hidden motivation came into view — I also knew myself as more than the motivation. When Sebastian Moore discovered his euphoria tape, he also discovered himself as more than that tape. When the secrets of the mind come into view and we see them, we are just a little more than what we see. We are the looker, not the looked at. The spiritual jargon is: anything we see is not ourselves. Can the eye see itself? Can the finger touch itself? We are always transcendent, not able to be reduced to what is known.

When we realize this truth about ourselves, we are close to the hidden treasure. We are in the territory of the soul, a spacious land that encompasses the realm of the mind and the body. In fact, the energies of the soul inform the mind and body and through them move into the outer world. In order to arrive at this soul we have reversed this inner to outer direction. We started with the outer and withdrew to the inner. We pulled back first from the outer world, then from the body, and finally from the mind. This pulling back was never a process of abandonment. We promised to return to the outer world. When we went beyond and became aware of the body, it was to set up a relationship with the body and allow the soul's energy to attend to it. When we became aware of the mind and therefore went beyond it, it was to set up a relationship with the mind and so allow the soul's energy to flood the mind. Consciousness is creating a mosaic, holding together the various aspects of the human. The space from which consciousness can do this is the soul space. This is now where consciousness rests. It is home base.

But it is only the midpoint in the journey. The treasure has yet to be discovered, and the return has yet to be undertaken.

A Map of the Spiritual World

When consciousness is in the soul space, there is an initial sense of emptiness. This sense of emptiness comes from the continual detachments that were necessary on the journey within. To some extent we identified with our roles and responsibilities in the outer world and with our bodies and minds in the inner world. As we moved beyond each of these realities, our identity was emptied of content. Although we stressed that each movement of transcendence produced a relationship with what was transcended, it also inevitably produced a sense of essential emptiness. This emptiness is the precondition for the entry of the Spirit.

Spirit is shy. It does not want to compete with other allegiances. It wants open spaces, vacancies that it can move into without conflict. When we are detached, we wait in readiness. The movement of transcendence that says adamantly again and again, "I am not this! I am not this!" is often promoted as a journey of increasing independence. Actually, it is a process of self-emptying, a becoming poor in order to be open for spiritual wealth, a giving-up that makes our hands empty and open. When we are like this, Spirit enters in gentleness, meekness, and love. The virgin's empty womb is filled with child. The empty tomb is filled with the presence of the resurrected Christ. As Meister Eckhart once put it, we are "pregnant with Nothingness."

My own image for this process is a "back door to the soul." The soul faces outward through the mind and body and into the world. Suddenly a door opens in the back of the soul, and Spirit enters. This image comes from a remark Chesterton made about Christmas. It was "rather as if a man had found an inner room in the very heart of his own house, which he had never suspected; and seen a light from within. It is as if he found something at the back of his own heart that betrayed him into good." In my imagination what is important is that it comes from the back. Spirit is not an object or person that can be seen. So it is not out in front to be observed, measured, described. I favor the sneak attack of a back door, suddenly opened by a combination of the soul's readiness and the Spirit's eagerness.

When soul opens to Spirit and at the same time remains open to mind, body, and outer world, its true nature is most evident. An ancient saying gives the soul two eyes: one peers into the temporal and one peers into the eternal. The idea is to keep both eyes open. This makes the soul essentially relational. We are the connective channel between the infinite Spirit and the finite mind, body, and world. This is the hidden treasure that was promised, a holy communion between Spirit, soul, and world. When we are awake to this communion, a series of realizations occurs.

First, there is the realization of essential participation. This is a subtle and crucial awareness. It is often described as a middle ground between identity and distance. When the soul opens to the profound and permeating influence of Spirit, sometimes the language of identity is used. "I am God" or "I am one with the divine" are statements many mystics are comfortable with. The union is so strongly and thoroughly perceived that there is a blurring of boundaries. Spirit and soul are identified. If mystics are tempted to this language of ecstatic union, ordinary people are tempted to the opposite language of distance. Creature and Creator are polar opposites. The Creator is omniscient, omnipotent, and immortal. The creature lacks knowledge and power and is mortal. The soul is most certainly the gift of God, but it is a gift that is given and then the Giver recedes. The creature has life from the Creator, but the Creator "watches at a distance." Soul is perceived as either "too close" to Spirit or "too far" from it.

My suggestion is that the realization of the soul space is not one of either identity or distance. It is a sense of essential participation, the awareness of an ongoing relationship with Spirit that establishes the reality of who we are. This is the true appreciation of creaturehood. To be a creature is not to focus on smallness and inadequacy. It is to know ourselves as indebted and grateful for the continual flow of life and love into us from the Spirit. We participate in the Divine Being at every moment. However, this truth is easily forgotten. The story of Solomon and the ant is a reminder.

> One day Solomon was in the sanctuary. An ant passed in front of him. He lifted his hand to throw the ant out of the sacred space.
>
> The ant protested, "Why do you intend to attack me? It is not your task to lay hands upon me in the house of God. Do not look on my smallness but the mystery of creation I

am. If I came out of this black robe so much divine splendor would radiate from my breast that all the monotheists of the world would be put to shame."

Of course, the principal monotheist to be put to shame is Solomon himself. He was about to sweep an ant out of God's house not knowing the ant *was* God's house. However, I am not sure this ant's ability to radiate divine splendor confounds monotheists as thoroughly as the story suggests. Although monotheism resists any hint of identity between creature and Creator, it does not demand an alienated distance. There is room for an immanent divine presence that radiates through all things. We are in a constant relationship with Spirit and therefore capable at any moment of revealing its power and love. This is the realization of essential participation.

A second realization is a sense of kinship and communion with all things. This realization goes against conventional expectations. It would seem that "going away" and "going within" would mean more distance and separation. The danger of this whole approach to spiritual consciousness is excessive individualism, even solipsism. In fact, this is often the reputation of the spiritual seeker: a lonely person in a lonely world seeking a lonely God. However, the richness of the directive "Know Yourself!" is becoming apparent. The self who is discovered is a completely relational being, in communion with God, neighbor, and earth.

The inner dynamics of this realization of holy communion is anchored in the previous realization of essential participation. When our consciousness remains tied to our social roles, bodies, and minds, our sense of self is well-defined and well within our skin boundaries. However, when we are in the soul space, we know ourselves in relationship to the Divine Source. What becomes apparent is that everything else is also related to this Divine Source. The God we find as the sustaining center of ourselves is the God who is always creating and sustaining all things. In Thomas Merton's famous religious experience in Louisville he realized he loved all the people he saw on the street. He knew none of them personally so his feeling of love was not on the personal and social levels. His lightning-flash conclusion was that there was no such thing as a separate holy existence. This is precisely the realization. Everything is interrelated. What is is inter-being. The Divine Source is love and love is the power "that drives everything there is toward everything else that is."

A third realization involves a heightened sense of discrepancy between the soul consciousness of participation and communion and the inner and outer worlds that are disordered, isolated, and violent. The way of spiritual consciousness has many twists and turns. The journey began with the enticement that we are something we do not know. Now we have found who we are at the deepest level. We know ourselves in biblical imagery as a child of God and brother or sister to all creation. However, as soon as we know this we also know we are not who we are. We are alienated from the reality of ourselves. This is the realization of sin. What must be stressed is the consciousness of alienation is dependent on the previous consciousness of participation. Only if we are connected to the Divine Source on one level can we perceive the separation from the Divine Source on other levels. In biblical theology the good creation is the background for the fall. Only the children of God know they live east of Eden.

Contemporary spirituality is often criticized for not focusing clearly enough on this predicament. Deeper levels of consciousness are used as a buffer against the harsh realities of mental anxieties, bodily suffering, and social alienation and conflict. Yet the most Western theological traditions have tried to live with the tension of simultaneously being related to God and alienated from God. The theological models used to hold these two perceptions together were not always persuasive. However, the twin themes — majesty and misery, dignity and dereliction, child of God and lost in the world — are a faithful reflection of soul consciousness. Also this realization sets the stage for the human adventure of redemption and is the initial indication of the divine-human mission. We have gone within and dwelled within. It is time to go without, to return to the "land of unlikeness" with the realizations of the soul space.

A fourth realization builds on and completes the realization of discrepancy. The nature of the Spirit which fills the emptiness of the soul is self-giving love. It is not thunder and lightning. It is a flow of fullness, gentle, unceasing, filling every open space and narrowed crevice. There is no scarcity in this self-giving, no hint that in its giving it is going to give out. Therefore, there is an ever increasing trust in its abundance. The more we give ourselves over to it, the more of it there is. This more does not crowd us out. The nature of this love is that it does not displace anything of what it enters into. It elevates, enhances, builds up what it communes with. Its purpose seems to be to make us all we can be. Because this is also our innermost dynamism we cooperate with its energies, open ourselves to its subtle movements. An inner transformation is under way.

Spiritual teachers stress that the more an image becomes like that which it images, the more it becomes itself. The more we allow the divine self-giving nature of God to permeate us, the more we take on the characteristics of that nature and join in its adventure. We begin to ride God into ourselves and into the world, joining in its mission of redemption and sanctification. We become a flow of life and love that is not our own. Spirit enters the mind and body and moves out into the world. The full truth of the spiritual journey is now revealed. It is a going within to go without. The ultimate goal is not communion with God but incarnation, making spirit flesh. Union with God is the first step, the necessary precondition for bringing God to the world. But mediating God into the world does not happen without resistance or difficulty.

In *Men and Angels* Mary Gordon constructs a small scene that, at least for me, captures a great deal of the difficulty of moving from the inside to the outside.* A woman is waiting for her children to come home from school. She positions herself next to the chair by the front window of the house. In this way she can see her children coming down the street. She can also have something to hold on to, for when she sees her children running down the street toward her, their coats undone, their school bags falling off

---

*Mary Gordon, *Men and Angels* (New York: Random House, 1985), 16.

their shoulders, a great love from the very center of her being begins to erupt. She needs the chair to steady herself, to keep from swooning. But when the children burst though the door, she says to them, "How was school?" "Was lunch all right?" "Did you have your math test?"

At one time or another we all feel great love in the center of ourselves, in the soul space as it opens and receives the love of the Spirit. This love explodes and pushes us into the outer world. However, the journey into the outer world must go through the labyrinth of the inner world. Love must be expressed through the mind and the body that have a history of conditionings. The swooning love comes out as motherly nagging. We are simultaneously in touch with divine abundance and human finitude and sin. We can feel the love that moves the sun and the stars and the worry over lunch and homework in the same breath. We are border people, touching divine love and human reluctance simultaneously.

So, in the last analysis, the spiritual life is about struggle. Perhaps Alfred North Whitehead's remark about Ulysses tells us the whole truth. Ulysses belonged to the gods and to the foxes. He participated in the worlds of inspiration and of cunning. Inspiration without cunning would have made him an angel. Cunning without inspiration would have rendered him an animal. The full human situation is a baffling mix of both.

There is one last aspect to this final realization that is crucial. The way of spiritual consciousness is to go within in order to go without. However, the paradox is when we go without, we also stay within. In other words, we enter the fray of the world without forgetting who we are. We remember the realizations of the soul space as we go about the work. As a result of the spiritual journey we have developed a dual consciousness. This means that no matter what we do we co-do it with the deeper Spirit of love that is pouring itself into the soul. In some strands of Christianity this is the fullness of the hidden treasure, the joining of contemplation and action, belonging to God and being in the world.

These maps of the outer, inner, and spiritual worlds are not the territory. This is the barest of sketches, skeletons without flesh. However, some sense of "going within to go without" is necessary if we are to appropriate the Jesus stories as guides to spiritual consciousness. The Jesus stories address many of the concerns of this spiritual journey:

- How people are lost in the outer world, seeking so many things that do not satisfy them and pinning their hopes on what fades.

- How when the soul and its Spirit grounding are not found, the mind, body, and outer world cannot be enjoyed. They are forced to do service as Spirit substitutes, and this distorts their capacity to give pleasure.

- How the mind both manufactures idols that block the way and creates symbols that open the way to spiritual consciousness.

- How we learn to love the body that gives us both pleasure and pain and the mind that both thrills and tortures us.

- How we fail again and again on the path of loving action. But no matter how frustrated we are, we do not give up for long.

- How the processes of detachment and attachment serve the Spirit-soul relationship.

- How prayer that keeps us in the soul space and action that keeps us engaged in the world live together.

However, before we explore specific Jesus stories, we must consider how to approach and appreciate them as resources for spiritual consciousness. We must learn how to allow them to show us the way within and the way without. We must make them our companions along the way.

Chapter 2

Telling Jesus Stories along the Way

On Not Telling Jesus Stories Straight

FOR TOO MANY YEARS NOW I have been telling stories to different groups of people. I have told stories at storytelling festivals, at religious education conferences, at health-care conventions, at academic gatherings, in retirement communities, during retreats and workshops and worship services of many different Christian denominations. Although the stories have entertainment value, I do not tell them for entertainment. Although many of the stories are humorous and people laugh at predictable places, guffaw is not the goal. Although the stories are often inspirational in the root sense of that word — breathing life into people — they are not chicken soup for the soul.

The stories I tell have spiritual ambitions. They are meant to evoke spirit, to bring the listener into the soul space, to enable the hearers to see their lives from a spiritual perspective. In order to do this stories help us get beyond established defenses, slow down the processes of judgment, and cultivate alternate perspectives. They pull hidden memories to the surface, encourage self-examination without condemnation, suggest levels of selfhood the dentist never sees, and document the detours that develop between intention and action. Stories also do many other things that cannot be predicted; but when they occur, they can be delighted in. All of these subtle psychological and spiritual movements are helpful in developing our birthright as people of spirit.

The stories I tell to activate spiritual potential come from everywhere. I tell stories from the spiritual traditions of the world — Buddhist, Hindu, Jewish, Sufi, Native American, Christian, etc.

45

I find contemporary stories in novels, autobiographies, memoirs, and the "snatches of experience" that are often tucked away in books of philosophy, theology, spirituality, and psychology. I have also polished and turned into tales the experiences that people have told me about (always with their permission). Finally, I have tried my hand and written stories that I hope have the power to evoke spirit. I am, in this regard, eclectic, gathering where I may and creating where I must. At times I worry about a certain recklessness in this approach. Do I ransack the treasures of the world's spiritual traditions? Yes, but with humility and respect, and never pretending to speak with any authority except the blend of ignorance and wisdom that at the moment emerges.

However, there is one criterion that I try to adhere to. I only tell stories that have first told me. When I listen to stories or read stories, I am often impressed or delighted or engaged. Although these are favorable experiences, something is missing. The story did not become intimate to me. It did not show me to myself or unfold for me a spiritual truth that brought me healing or an increased desire for life. The story did not have "my name on it." As good as it was, for some reason it was not mine. Consequently, after hearing or reading it, I felt no drive to tell it. Tellers tell what first told them. And so the stories I tell, be they from other faiths and cultures or part of my own life experience, are known to me because they first knew me. If Augustine was right and God is more intimate to us than we are to ourselves, these stories also know God and live in that elusive space where the divine and human spirits interact.

Therefore, I try to tell only what I know. Of course, this does not mean that I have exhausted the richness of any particular story or that my understanding is the "right one." The story is always more than the storyteller, both objectively as a pre-existing narrative and subjectively in its ability to evoke multiple responses in the listeners. It only means that I have a piece of the action. I am not a mindless teller, a repeater of tales, a complete mimic of another's art. Hindu literature uses a suggestive image for people's relationship to scripture. "Many are like the donkey who carries sandalwood. They know the burden, but not the fragrance." I try not to be the donkey, struggling under a weight without a whiff of its intoxicating perfume. I know some of the scent of the stories I tell.

There is one disconcerting exception to what I have said. The stories that have influenced me most, the ones I know best, the ones that pop up even in casual conversations, the ones that have so profoundly showed me to myself that I cannot talk about myself for long without telling these stories — these stories I do not tell.

I do not tell stories of Jesus.

I Missed It

I will be telling stories to a group and someone will say, "Tell us some Jesus stories."

Without missing a beat, I usually respond, "This one you won't find in the gospels, but what it makes you consider you might find in the gospels."

Then I tell folk tales about Jesus or midrash stories about Jesus (stories that use the gospel narratives as a base and then spin off in another direction, introducing new characters and plots or continuing the adventures of a minor gospel character). For some reason I am reluctant to tell gospel stories straight, to just "stand and deliver." I have often heard others tell gospel stories. From the point of view of a storyteller's art some have told them well and some have told them poorly. Many have added details and motivations that are not in the original story. Others have conflated parallel stories from the four gospels into a single mishmash tale. All of this is fair game, if you know what you are doing.

There is a Jesus story that did not make it into all the manuscripts of Luke's gospel. "Jesus saw a man performing a work on the Sabbath. He said to him, 'Man, if you know what you are doing, you are blessed. But if you do not know what you are doing, you are cursed.'" In search of blessing rather than curse I have tried to find out what I am doing. More precisely, what I am *not* doing. Where does my reluctance comes from? Why am I hesitant to tell the stories straight?

Certainly some of it comes from my upbringing. Although as a small child I heard the gospel stories read and at times told, that was not my major or sustaining contact with them. I started meditating on the gospels when I was fourteen. Whatever else meditation is, it is not a quick process. It is a slow push into each word, a dwelling in the text, a waiting for its gift to be opened, a start-distraction-restart engagement of affect and intelligence. With this background of silence and leisurely contemplation, telling a gospel story or listening to one always strikes me as too fast. I cannot get into it because deep down I am saying, "Whoa! Slow down!" I feel I am gulping my food.

Although this "slow down" instinct is in me, I believe it also does justice to the stories. The stories are both sparse and dense. Their very compactness makes them difficult to tell. They happen too fast for the ear, at least an ear that has only one try at them. It seems to me the gospel stories are crafted jewels. They must be held up to the light and turned slowly. In this way their radiance shines forth. Each twist and turn, each nuance is appreciated. When they are told straight, storytellers are burdened to bring out this subtlety in their craft. And the listeners have to be alert, tracking every line, swaying with each syllable. I have heard the saying, "Pull your chair up to the edge of the precipice and let me tell you a story." That is the level of alertness that is needed in the listener to "hear and get" a gospel story.

Consider: In Matthew's story of the Canaanite woman, she initially confronts Jesus with this combination of titles, "Lord, Son of David, have mercy on me." (This story of the Canaanite woman will be the "example story" for this chapter.) This is a complete and accurate designation of Jesus. He is the Lord and therefore meant for everyone. He is also the Son of David, a Jew, a particular man from a particular people. As the story unfolds, it becomes clear that Jesus is refusing to talk to her because she is not a Jew. His mission is only to the "lost sheep of the *house of Israel.*" So in their next interaction, she comes forward and does him homage saying, "Help me, Lord!" She has dropped the title Son of David. There is no advantage in reminding Jesus he is a Jew. It is precisely because he is a Jew that he is ignoring her. Therefore, the burden of the storyteller is to try to make this omission significant in the telling and the burden of the listener to catch this "title word play." The demands on both teller and hearer are considerable.

Consider: In Luke's story we call "The Prodigal Son" the younger son squanders his inheritance and falls to feeding the pigs. In this condition of wanting to eat what they fed the pigs but "no one gave him anything," he comes to his senses. The story-teller than treats us to his inner monologue, "How many of my father's hired servants have bread enough and to spare, but I perish here with hunger! I will arise and go to my father and I will say to him, 'Father, I have sinned against heaven and before you. I am no longer worthy to be called your son. Treat me as one of your hired hands.'" This is the script the son creates in the pig pen.

However, after his father, seeing him from afar and having compassion, runs to him, embraces him, and kisses him, this is what he says: "Father, I have sinned against heaven and before you. I am no longer worthy to be called your son." He drops the line, "Treat me as one of your hired hands." Could this be backpedaling? He is already in the embrace of the father. Why stress the penalty for his squandering? Is this an important omission to notice? I think it is. But how is the storyteller going to stress it and how is the listener, poised for subtlety, going to be able to remember and contrast the script from the pig pen with the script in the embrace of the father? A problem for both teller and listener.

Consider: In John's story of the woman at the well Jesus says, "If you knew the gift of God and who is saying to you, 'Give me a drink,' you would ask him and he would give you living water." This complex line structures the rest of the exchange between Jesus and woman. First, he leads her to understand the gift of God; then he reveals to her who it is who is saying to her, "Give me a drink." But it is difficult for the teller to show how this line shapes the entire dialogue, and it is difficult for the listener to catch the connection. Perhaps that is why John at one point says, "These things are *written* that you may believe...."

Perhaps the stories have to be read. Only in this way can we appreciate their subtlety. Or perhaps they can be told, but not in a traditional "stand and deliver" way. Perhaps their structure and their ultimate purpose — to communicate the spirit of Jesus — suggest a different way of communication.

I Already Heard It

"What stories are you going to tell this afternoon?"

The question came from a boy of about ten. His father had walked him up to me and encouraged, "Go on. Ask him."

It was at a Family Life Conference in Toledo. In the morning I had told family stories, and I was booked for another session in the afternoon. The kids could either go to hear me or sing songs with Joe Wise. The boy needed to make a decision, but he wanted more information.

"I was going to tell Jesus stories, but that does not mean . . . "

I did not have to go any further.

"Well, I suppose I've heard them, haven't I? I think I'll go with Joe."

Wise choice (pun intended)!

This is the second reason why I do not tell Jesus stories straight. Most of the people I tell stories to are Christians. A large percentage of these are regular churchgoers. They have heard the gospel stories many times. Protestants often cite chapter and verse. Although I have learned how to do this, it still makes me a little nervous. Too much knowledge is being displayed. With my Catholic upbringing I am more comfortable saying, "We usually read that one during Lent — or is it Advent?" But either way — with Protestant precision or Catholic liturgical latitude — the stories have been heard.

This makes me reluctant to tell it one more time. I know the standard response is to cite the story-greedy kid who for the thousandth time asks his mother to tell him the story of "The Three Bears" or "The Little Engine That Could." But we could also take a long look at the story-weary face of the mother who, out of love or duty or just to get the kid to sleep, is going to tell it one more time. The kid may settle in for pleasure but, chances are, the adult will be close to comatose. It is difficult to hear a story over and over again and have it be fresh, exciting, and generative of insights. In pastoral and theological circles it is often said we must tell the parables of Jesus so that we are "once more astonished." Be my guest. Give it a try.

However, there is a strange twist to people's familiarity with gospel stories. They have encountered these stories in Bible schools, religion classes, preaching and teaching situations. They have heard the stories and heard the stories interpreted. What sticks is the interpretation, the meaning, the theme, the lesson. The characters, the dialogue, the sequence of events, and the crucial turns of plot are often vague and sometimes hilariously confused. Over the years I have had to break the news to people that Mary Magdalene did not dance with Jesus at the wedding feast of Cana, angels did not sing at the death of Christ, and Jesus did not walk out of the tomb. Turnabout being eminently fair play, people have had to break the news to me that Simeon and Anna are *not* in Matthew's gospel, Mary Magdalene *is* at the tomb in Mark's gospel, and (to move for a moment into the Hebrew scriptures) it was Reuben *and* Judah who persuaded the other brothers not to kill Joseph. Ouch!

Although we have heard the stories many times, what we remember is a plot summary or a point. These attached meanings are all that remain and sometimes they are far from "the family of insights" that careful attention to the story would generate. In one class I taught with graduate theological students there was a vigorous discussion of the second creation story in Genesis, the Adam and Eve story. After much talk about what it meant and various lines from the story being cited, I asked if anyone could tell the story. A few ventured plot summaries — "It is about..." No one knew the story as a story.

I believe familiarity with gospel stories suffers from the same vagueness. People have heard the story and an attendant interpretation. When they hear the story again, the interpretation comes to the forefront of their consciousness and swallows the concreteness of the story. If there is a path to being once more astonished by gospel stories, it is to temporarily disconnect the inherited meaning from the actual narrative. Then by careful attention to the actual flow of the story, new insights may emerge. A possible appraisal might be, "I heard that story, but I never heard it that way."

Religious educators tell me that a new situation is emerging. People, especially young people, have not heard the gospel stories. This may point to a regrettable lack of socialization into the Christian community and tradition. But it is also an opportunity. Who knows what a young adult may perceive on hearing these stories for the first time?

I Don't Get It

"You know what I never got was...why the father didn't explain more to the older son...why the workers hired last got the same...why Jesus didn't defend himself at the trial...why Jesus was so hard on Nicodemus...why Jesus delayed in going to see his sick friend Lazarus...why Jesus called Peter Satan...why Jesus vanished after he broke the bread...why the Messiah had to suffer...why...why...why..."

A common experience of most people is not to "get" gospel stories. It is not clear what motivates the characters, why the plot turns in precisely that way, or why the storyteller interrupts the narrative to tell the reader a certain piece of information. A lot of this "not getting it" has to do with unfamiliar literary conventions, different cultural assumptions, lost historical contexts, and not remembering the overall theological drive of the narrative. The more we know about the literary, cultural, and historical trappings of the gospels the better off we are. When scholars light the way, our chances of "getting it" greatly increase.

However, there may be another and deeper reason for chronic puzzlement about gospel stories. These stories are written from a spiritual consciousness, and we are most at home in a conventional consciousness. When stories do not immediately make sense to us, there may be nothing wrong with the story. It may be that our ability to receive the story is diminished because we are not on the same wave length as the story. A spiritual story is being heard with conventional ears. We have ears, but hear not; eyes, but see not. Or, in the archaic English translation of the Markan Jesus' rebuke of Peter, we "mindest not the things of God, only of men." We don't get it!

It may be a question of developing what in later Christian spirituality will be called spiritual senses. As the physical senses enable us to perceive and receive the material world, the spiritual senses enable us to perceive and receive the spiritual world. Of course, the material and the spiritual are not two separate tracks. Following a standard theology of incarnation John Chrysostom exclaimed, "On every side all things commingle!" Therefore, attending to the spiritual is not a matter of sorting it out from messy matter. It is a depth discernment of spirit as it sustains and transforms the material world. What is necessary is to put the physical eye within the spiritual eye, or as e.e. cummings once phrased it after the fact, "the eye of my eye was opened."

The parable of the sower as it appears in Mark (4:1–20) and Matthew (13:1–23) provides a clue to this movement from conventional to spiritual consciousness. Jesus tells the parable twice. The first time he tells it straight without any interpretation: "A sower went out to sow. And as he sowed, some seeds fell along the path and the birds came and devoured them...." After this telling, Jesus has a conversation with his disciples. He contrasts those outside whose "ears are heavy of hearing and whose eyes are closed" with those inside whose eyes and ears are "blessed." Those outside hear the story but they do not get it. Therefore, they are not able to "turn," to change their mind, to see the hidden meaning of the parable. But to those inside, the disciples, Jesus is going to give "the secrets of the kingdom of heaven." In other words, he is going to reveal the hidden, spiritual meaning of the observable events of the parable.

Jesus then decodes the sower, the seeds, and various types of soils. He tells the story disclosing its inner significance: "When anyone hears the word of the kingdom and does not understand it, the evil one comes and snatches away what is sown in his heart. This is what was sown along the path." The material images of the story are now interpreted from a spiritual point of view. This two-layer possibility, story as conundrum or story as spiritual insight, may be applicable to more than just the parable of the sower. As Jesus says in Mark, "Do you not understand this parable? How then will you understand all the parables?" This may mean: as the sower-seed-soil parable is about how the seed is received differently by different soil so all the parables of Jesus are about how his revelation will be received. Or it may mean that all the parables, and by extension many of the gospel stories, work on two levels. The surface level is a story about the perils of farming; the depth level is a story about the perils of soul. Awakened eyes and ears are necessary to move from the surface to the depth, from the circumference to the center, from the outside to the inside.

Talk of the gospel stories containing "secrets" or "hidden meanings" or being accessible only to those on the "inside" makes people nervous. It smacks of elitism and esotericism. It will only breed another "in" group, haughty and self-righteous. Also when we move in this direction, how far away are we from cults and bizarre predictions about the future? The perennial Christian game of the "damned and the saved" will be played on a new field. People will be consigned to "exterior darkness where there is weeping and gnashing of teeth" not only because of moral wrongdoing but also because of spiritual obtuseness. Is this another fearsome rendition of the narrow path of salvation? When the blind lead the blind, both fall into the pit. When the seeing lead the blind, is there inevitable domination and division? If spiritual consciousness is linked to uncovering the deeper meanings of texts, there has to be a great deal of "careful walking."

However, it is good to keep in mind that spiritual seeing is a human potential. It is standard Christian anthropology that each person is ensouled. Therefore, the "eye of the soul" can be opened. We can learn to see more or less clearly from that perspective. As with all human potentials, it is more highly developed in some people than in others. In that baffling blend of nature and nurture, some people gravitate to developing spiritual gifts. It is my assumption that the gospel writers were such people. They were highly developed spiritually, and they crafted stories, in the memory and style of Jesus, that were meant to communicate spiritual truth. Our effort is to attune ourselves to their art so that we may receive their gift. When the incognito risen Christ walked with the two disciples on the road to Emmaus, he opened the scriptures for them. The result was their hearts burned and their eyes saw. Is not this the ultimate reason we read sacred writings?

When spiritual insight is communicated through a sacred story, it is often accompanied by a strange realization. When we first encounter the story and "we don't get it," we are sure the problem is with the story. It was ineptly copied or something crucial was lost in transmission or the writer was not skilled enough or the story is not sophisticated enough for the twists and turns of the contemporary mind. When the breakthrough happens and we get it, the story appears luminous, transparent, undeniable. It is then we realize where the veil was. The veil was not in the story but on our eyes. The story did not have a hidden meaning. We had closed sensibilities. Spiritual truth is hidden in plain sight. We are just not used to looking. Spiritual consciousness is waking up to what is there. The stories are illumined guides, and we are unillumined, stumbling along the way.

For these three reasons — compactness, familiarity, and spiritual strangeness — I do not tell the Jesus stories straight. However, I do tell them. Exactly how I tell them is the result of how I learned them or, more accurately, how they showed me to myself. Every storyteller must make the story her or his own. With the stories of Jesus this is an especially difficult endeavor and ultimately a profound mystery of transformation. For me it is enigmatically captured in an aphorism of Meister Eckhart: "Our bodily food is changed into us, but our spiritual food changes us into itself."

On Making Jesus Stories Our Own

I learned a great deal about approaching the gospels from the pitfalls of preaching. For thirty years I preached every Sunday. One of the three touchstone texts was always from the gospels.

There were few Saturdays when I was not on a "homily hunt." As the preaching time approached, I would be staring at the gospel story, hoping something would "pop out" and catapult me toward seven to ten minutes of insight and inspiration. I learned first hand a truth of interpretation: "Those who come to plunder are turned away." The story would not cooperate. If it had riches, they were hidden behind closed doors. I did not have the key.

This utilitarian approach — "You only come by when you want something" — is deadly. We are not apprenticing ourselves to the story. We are using the story as part of an ecclesial task or a teaching assignment or for making a point in an article or book. At a preaching workshop someone asked, "If you did not have to preach, would you be spending your time studying and meditating on the gospels?" In other words, "Would you be a serious follower of Jesus if you were not a preacher in the church?" The gospels are a gift for our own personal spiritual development. If we would respect this, we would open them with that primarily in mind — at least some of the time.

Over the years I have found myself doing "repeated things" in order to open a gospel story. To appreciate its wisdom I come back again and again to certain "moves." I *study* the story, *meditate* on its spiritual truths, and *integrate* its wisdom into my life. Each of these areas breaks down into a number of "sub-moves," things I do while I am studying, meditating, and integrating. For the purpose of order I will explore these areas one at a time, but in actuality they overlap and there is no preferred or set sequence. I suppose all this, and more, is contained in the classical approach to scripture texts — *lectio* (reading), *meditatio* (meditation), *oratio* (prayer), *contemplatio* (contemplation), *operatio* (action). However, because of personality type or laziness or intellectual propensity I shuttle back and forth between the three realms of study, meditation, and integration.

Study

Many Bibles are not eye-friendly. The print is too small and packed into two parallel columns on one page. The formatting is often dense, not conducive to following the narrative flow. There are not enough paragraph breaks and the dialogue is not set apart. The eye is presented with a block of print to be penetrated. Uncovering the spiritual wisdom of a text is formidable enough. There is no need for the "look" of the story to be an obstacle.

I also have some quibbles with translations (who doesn't?). I like literal translations, the closer to the Greek the better. If, for example, in John 20 the Greek says he "was in the middle of them," I do not appreciate he "stood before them." Or in Luke 7 if the Greek says, "Behold a woman," I do not appreciate "There came a woman." I do not want beautiful, flowing English prose. I want clunky transliterations. The reason is that I suspect the language with its deliberate repetitions and positionings may be a clue to the breakthrough in consciousness embodied in the story. It is a wager, but, at least in one theory, all interpretation begins as a gamble.

Therefore, the first thing that I do is lift the story out of the Bible, type it out, basically but not exclusively using the translation of the RSV Interlinear Greek-English New Testament. It looks something like this.

Jesus was walking along the borders of Tyre and Sidon.

Behold a Canaanite woman, living in those borders, coming forward, crying out, "Lord, Son of David, have mercy on me. My daughter is terribly troubled by a demon."

He gave her no word of response.

His disciples entreated him, "Get rid of her. She keeps shouting after us."

Jesus replied, "My mission is only to the lost sheep of the house of Israel."

She came forward and did him homage, saying, "Help me, Lord."

"It is not right," said Jesus, "to take the food that is meant for the children and throw it to the dogs."

"Yes, Lord," she replied. "But even the dogs eat the scraps that fall from the master's table."

"O woman," said Jesus, "great is your faith. Be it done for you as you desire."

That very moment her daughter got better.

With the story in place I next consult the scholars: standard commentaries, *New Testament Abstracts,* various New Testament dictionaries, and, if possible, writings from mystics and theologians that focus on this story. I am not a scripture scholar but, as with most people who have preached and/or taught Christian faith, I am a voracious consumer of scripture scholarship.

Over the years I have settled into a double sentiment about what I have consumed. First, I am appreciative and grateful. There is so much to know and so many women and men have scrutinized these ancient texts and uncovered their intricate workings and complex connections. Learning from them is always a pleasure. Second, these scholarly efforts are not a substitute for personal engagement. They are a beginning, positioning the spiritual seeker on the Jesus path. However, in order for some illumination to occur there must be creative interaction with the text. Spiritual development is not a second-hand enterprise. We cannot borrow it from the bright. We can only slowly apprentice ourselves to the emerging wisdom of the story, sitting at the feet of the story-Christ.

There are multiple scholarly approaches to the gospels. All of them are interesting and have complementary contributions to make. I divide them into two overly general categories: historical and literary. The historical approaches supply information about the "behind the text" context for the story. Did this happen in the ministry of Jesus? What was the situation in the early Christian community that provoked this story? Is there historically reliable Jesus material in this episode? How are the culture and times of Jesus reflected in the story?

The literary approaches stay more "within the text," focusing on the literary form and making connections with ever larger contexts and themes. What is the formal structure of this particular literary form? How does this story fit into the overall intent of the gospel writer? Do the characters in the story appear elsewhere?

Are they representative of theological or social positions? What attitudes do the characters display and are those attitudes complimented or confronted? What is the reader being led to consider by the structure of the story? Does the story assume a certain mindset in the reader/listener? As a storyteller I gravitate to the literary explorations. I will bring in historical information when it is needed and helpful. The historical is a back-up to my primary approach of attending to setting, character, and plot.

However, the literary approach is not an end in itself. The literary is at the service of the spiritual. I am looking for the "spiritual logic" that connects the sentences, in particular the connections between the dialogue of the key players. Tracing the spiritual spine of the story entails asking a series of questions. In Matthew's story of the Canaanite woman why does Jesus give her "no word of response"? What is the function of the disciples' saying, "Get rid of her. She keeps shouting after us"? How is what Jesus says to the disciples a reply to what they have said? How does the verbal jousting about dogs, houses, tables, and food change the flow of the exchange between Jesus and the woman? What does Jesus see in the woman that prompts him to exclaim that she has great faith? Why is the cure immediate? In other words, how does the story hang together and unfold? And, in particular, what does it tell us about the way of spiritual consciousness, the movement within and the flow without?

The answers to these questions begin the formation of an alternative spiritual language and a symbolic understanding of the people, places, and things involved. This process moves the story toward universal application. It is not just a tale of a past historical encounter of Jesus with the Canaanite woman. It is a symbolic account of differences coming together and being overcome. The exact way the meeting and transcending occur is the path of spiritual wisdom. This is the spiritual teaching of the story. The stories may be about past peoples, but they are also about present possibilities. The connection between the past and present is through the spiritual wisdom that emerges from the story when it is approached with literary and symbolic sensitivities.

Too often study and meditation have been separated when

dealing with gospel stories. When we study, we stay distanced from the text and treat it like an object under observation. When we pray, we springboard off the text without regard for the rigorous insights that study supplies. I begin with study, knowing I will not end there. When the spiritual wisdom begins to emerge, a second phase of making the Jesus story our own is beginning.

Meditation

It is difficult to say how spiritual wisdom emerges in the mind. On one level, it is the result of careful attention to the story and patiently abiding with its flow. On another level, the advent of the wisdom is a gift. It seems to arrive on its own. I always take this to mean, perhaps naively, that it has been prompted by the deeper dimension of spirit. The spirit of the text has awakened my spirit. It has stirred my mind to see and understand. I begin to see with the eye of the soul. This type of seeing is distinguished from seeing with the eye of the flesh which discerns discrete objects, the flow of separate entities. It is also distinguished from seeing with the eye of the mind, which bunches separate entities into groups and then contrasts, compares, and relates them. The eye of the soul is different from these two eyes, but it does not bypass them. The eye of the soul informs, elevates, and perfects the eye of the mind and the eye of the flesh. It allows them to appreciate the spiritual dimension of what they perceive. When the eye of the soul floods the eye of the mind and the eye of the flesh, it feels in retrospect like a darkness has been illumined. We are, if only for a moment, enlightened. The result is spiritual wisdom.

Also a different language begins to be shaped. When we are studying the story, we use the language of the story. We puzzle over the exchanges of Jesus, the disciples, and the Canaanite woman. This story language is concrete and specific. When the spiritual wisdom emerges, the language becomes more general. It sounds more like a spiritual teaching or a theological reflection. We are now considering a common condition rather than a specific instance, and so naturally the language becomes more general. The wisdom emerging from the story of Jesus and the Canaanite woman begins to sound like this.

"We have many identities. Some are more inclusive than others. Often we cling to our narrower identities. We glory in the fact we are a man instead of a woman, a Jew instead of a Gentile, six foot two instead of five foot six. When we cling to these identities, we set up boundaries that either intentionally or unintentionally exclude people. However, we have a deeper identity, a 'Lord' identity, as the story puts it. This identity is the image of God in us and makes us brother and sister to all others who share this image. When we glory in this dimension of ourselves, we overcome the boundaries that our other identities create. When these boundaries are transcended, the mercy that was stanched by the narrower identities is released. I wonder if this is the case: when we widen our identity, mercy flows."

It is also my intent to put the new language forward as tentative probings, explorations that may or may not have merit. The reason for this is that I think the ultimate validation of this spiritual wisdom will be personal. Does it illumine our experiences and point to "things" we have dimly surmised and now can see more clearly? Although the Jesus story has generated this spiritual wisdom and hopefully the wisdom is a decent accounting of the story, no argument is put forward that this is the correct interpretation of the story. Nor at this time is it asserted that this theological or spiritual perspective is faithful to the major themes of the Christian tradition. These concerns will be addressed "as we walk along." All that is now said is this: "How does this speak to you? Is it part of your experience? Does it smack of truth to you?" In other words, the wisdom is an invitation to experience. If we accept the invitation, we move into the third phase.

Integration

At one point I thought of calling this third phase the treasuring of wisdom. That phrase would resonate with some gospel passages. It might call to mind the treasure in the field for which we sell everything. In this way it would highlight the "valuable-

ness" of the teaching. If the phrase connected with Matthew's
maxim "Where your treasure is, there will your heart be also,"
it might evoke the question of commitment. But my own appreciation of the word "treasuring" and my temptation to use it came
after I saw the implications of Luke's stating twice in his infancy
narrative that Mary "treasured" these things in her heart.

At first glance there is an interesting inconsistency in Luke's infancy narrative. When Gabriel appears to the aged Zachary and
tells him that he is soon to be a father, Zachary responds, "How
shall I know this? For I am an old man and my wife is advanced
in years." Gabriel is not happy with this response. He reminds
Zachary, "I am Gabriel who stands in the presence of God. I
was sent to speak to you and bring you this good news." Free
paraphrase: "Let's get things straight. I represent the power of
God and I'm on a mission to tell you what God is doing. And
your only reaction is to doubt if it can happen?" Zachary is
then silenced until the birth he did not think could happen has
come about.

But when Gabriel tells Mary she is to become the mother of
the Son of the Most High, she says something very similar to
Zachary, "How can this be, since I know not man?" However,
Mary is not silenced. She is given an explanation — a mystical explanation, but still an explanation. "The Holy Spirit will
come upon you and the power of the Most High will overshadow
you." Both Zachary and Mary have questions about the possibility of what the angel has predicted. How is it that Zachary is
silenced and Mary is given the favorable treatment of an explanation? Is this reverse gender discrimination? This is the seeming
inconsistency.

However, a closer look at the conversation between Mary and
Gabriel reveals that Mary's question is her second response to the
angel's good news. When the angel arrives, he greets her, "Hail,
O highly favored one! The Lord is with you." Her response to
this salutation is to be troubled and to consider in her mind what
the greeting meant. Mary is a ponderer of what she does not immediately understand. Zachary's doubt effectively dismisses the
angel's message; Mary entertains his troublesome words, trouble-

some because they do not easily fit into Mary's way of thinking. By the time she asks her question it is not to doubt the message but to figure out what she must do to cooperate with it. She is trying to integrate the higher wisdom of the angel into her existing mental categories. Even further, she is inquiring about how to enact the word she is hearing. The proper response to higher wisdom is pondering and treasuring what you are only beginning to understand.

Luke stresses this pondering/treasuring activity of Mary. When the shepherds make known what the angel told them and how they found the child, "all who heard it were amazed." But not Mary. "She kept all these things, treasuring them in her heart." After the episode of losing and finding the boy Jesus in the temple, Luke tells us, "his mother treasured these things in her heart." Mary lives between the dismissal of Zachary and the amazement of the crowds. Therefore, within the gospels themselves, there is the clue on how to receive its higher spiritual wisdom. Do not play Zachary and dismiss it out of hand because it does not fit within your conventional categories. Do not play the shepherds and be mindlessly amazed by it. Play Mary and take it into your heart and treasure it.

Later in the gospel Luke further explores this idea of treasuring. In Jesus' explanation of the parable of the sower the good soil that yields a hundredfold are those "who, hearing the word, hold it fast in an honest and good heart, and bring forth fruit in patience" (Luke 8:15). To me this describes the process of integration. "Holding it fast" points to the difficulty of turning a fleeting insight into a steady form of seeing. It is one thing to have a moment of illumination; it is quite another thing to see persistently from a spiritual point of view. This "ongoing holding" has to be done in an "honest and good heart." The heart is the deepest center of the person. It is the soul space that is the core of spiritual consciousness, the space that in the back (so to speak) opens into the infinite world of spirit and in the front (so to speak) flows in mind, body, and out into the world.

This space is a place of both honesty and goodness. The thousand ways we deceive ourselves have to be recognized and released. There has to be an acknowledgement of the truth of the human condition. The foolishness of clinging to the perishing forms of physical and social life must be confronted with clear eyes. This honest appraisal is the prerequisite for goodness. The good heart enacts the wisdom it is beginning to understand. The good follows the true. But the producing of this good fruit will take place in patience. Spiritual transformation from the center of the self to the circumference, from the depth to the surface, from the inside to the outside is not cosmetic change. It is the integration of spiritual wisdom into a conflicted mind and a knotted body, and then through a series of endless experiments into a world of faithfulness and deceit.

There is an instructive incident in Nikos Kazantzakis's autobiography, *Report to Greco*. He is walking quickly through the woods, rushing to get to a village. He comes upon a cocoon that is partially split open. He wants to see the final transformation, the emergence of the butterfly, but he is in a hurry. So he puts the cocoon under his mouth and blows his hot breath into the opening until the chrysalis completely opens. A beautiful butterfly wings up into the air. It is a feast for Kazantzakis's eye, but only for a moment. The butterfly shrivels, dies, and falls to the ground. Kazantzakis tried to rush a birth and inadvertently brought about a death. The process bears forth fruit, but only in patience.

The language of integration is often personal. We tell how we resisted the teaching or failed to understand it because we were afraid or attached to another way of thinking. We disclose our gradual gains in spiritual perception and our tentative and often disastrous attempts to apply it. It is a story of struggle. It is often accompanied by the realization that we are not Jesus. We are not other Christs. We are other Peters, Jameses, disciples, Pharisees, Sadducees, high priests, etc. We are all the characters in the gospels except the towering main player. Our rush to imitate Christ may have kept us from following him. "And they were on the road, going up to Jerusalem, and Jesus was walking ahead of them. They were amazed and those who followed him were afraid" (Mark 10:32). Not a heroic picture, but an honest one.

A good way to connect the phases of study, meditation, and

integration is through language. During the study phase the language is story-tied, analyzing character and mapping out plots. There is a lot of Jesus, disciple, and adversary talk. In the meditative phase a language develops that is story-indebted but not story-tied. The Jesus-disciple-adversary language fades out. In its place is the more general language of spiritual teaching and theological reflection. Through the phase of integration this language unfolds into the words of personal struggle. Personal storytelling is now added to the Jesus story and its developed spiritual wisdom to complete the process of making the Jesus story our own.

On Offering the Jesus Stories to Others

Since I was a child, people have offered me Jesus stories. My mother and father passed them along. The teachers in the school and the priest in the pulpit shouted and whispered them to me. Books told me the stories, the authors twisting them according to their own experience and insight. Friends have shared Jesus stories and the stories' impact on them. I have never received a Jesus story without someone else coming along with it. As was mentioned, even the gospels are passed along with Matthew, Mark, Luke, and John as companions. It seems to be the way it is in time and history. We never get Jesus without the fingerprints of those who have handled him.

Not all of these offerings have been on the same level, and I have not received them with the same interest or passion. Some of them seemed to be deeper, more profound, dazzling me with a vision beyond what I could imagine. I sat with those offerings. I used to say, "There is no use having a God idea unless it blows your mind." And when an offering blew my mind, I would stay with it as I picked up the pieces and put them into a larger mosaic. In this regard I have had many teachers. Some I have known personally and some I have only met through print or film. They offered me Christ and themselves. I ate what I had an appetite for. But I thank them all for their offerings.

I cannot prove this historically, but I like to imagine that it was something like this in the early church. Certain people had been with Jesus and through their contact with him had learned his mind. He gave them ears to hear and eyes to see. He offered to them the kingdom of God. The hook — and it became apparent only too quickly — was that they had to offer the kingdom of God to others. They did this by telling the story of the One who offered the kingdom of God to them. Eventually these stories were written down, but these writings had "large spaces" between the lines. The teller of the tale amplified it by careful attention (study), spiritual wisdom (meditation), and personal witness (integration). All three languages were part of the offering.

In this way the already initiated and developed became a living offering to the uninitiated and the undeveloped. Gospel storytelling was most often an interactive event between leadership and community. A leader is someone who is further along in having the mind of Christ than others in the community. Her role is to give others the mind of Christ as she understands it. She does this by apprenticing them to the same stories that were used to apprentice her. She is giving as she has received. The question always is: how is this to be done? She has made the Jesus story her own. How does she offer it to others?

This "offering to others" is not arbitrary. It is essential to the spiritual wisdom imparted through the Jesus stories. The stories make it clear over and over again. Anything that is received must be given away. Once the Spirit has been given to one person, giving the Spirit away to others is the proper response. Of course, this can be done in many ways. Our focus is on how people receive and give away the stories. So as long as imagination has taken me this far, I might as well allow it to unfold further. Let us picture one way the stories are offered to others.

※

People are gathering in a house. They greet one another, small talk for openers, a detail-by-detail sorting and shifting of the day's affairs. Eventually without much direction they arrange themselves in a circle. Silence comes naturally. As they sit together, they settle into themselves. If there was previously rush or hurry, a frantic step or a racing mind, it is disappearing now. Soon there will be words but not until the silence has emptied the mind. The soil for the seed needs to be tilled.

One of the group begins to speak. She is initiating things and throughout the meeting, which will last about an hour and a half, she will guide the conversation. Before she spoke, she would not have been picked out as the leader. There was no special deference paid to her. She did not carry herself in an "important" way. The "air of authority" was missing. All the time she will speak, there will be no muscle in her voice. She will not argue or ridicule or defend or rebut. She will speak simply and clearly, helping others to see what has become visible to her.

As the others listen to her, they will find themselves paying attention. However, it will not be an effort; the strain of attending will be strangely missing. At first it will not be obvious why her voice, which does not use any vocal or dramatic tricks, is so compelling. Only later will they realize what was missing was the tension the ego brings to everything we say and do. Her ego was present, yet she spoke from some place beyond ego. And her words awakened that place within them. Restful yet incredibly alert.

She speaks of what she knows. And when she speaks of what she does *not* know, she says, "I do not know this of myself, but others have told me and I think their word is trustworthy. Their life is compassionate, and what they say in full bloom I know within myself as a seed. And so I tell you their words in my words. And they tell me that their words, although they are their own, go back to Jesus' words."

The secret is out. She is both an apprentice and a master. She will give a teaching to this group, yet she herself has been taught and is still in the process of learning. She is a follower of the spiritual wisdom of Jesus, but she did not know Jesus in the flesh. She has known others and those others knew others who knew still others who, eventually and at last, knew Jesus. But whatever Jesus is, he is not a substitute for his followers. They are themselves, yet fashioned in his image. Their memory of him and his presence augments them. To put on his mind, they do not lose their own. His mind lifts their minds to a higher place where they can see more clearly. This is the nature of Jesus' self-giving. In turn their minds lift other minds and the tradition and wisdom of Jesus is continued.

She begins. She tells the whole story of the Canaanite woman. She tells it slowly, pausing between the lines. Although her voice is appropriate to the story, she is not performing. She is speaking the words from a deep space inside her. During the silence her consciousness settled in that space and it remains there as she speaks. When she finishes the story, she suggests that everyone be patient with themselves and the story.

"Let us return to the beginning." Now the story will be unpacked and decoded. The spiritual dynamics of the story will be honored.

Jesus was walking along the borders of Tyre and Sidon.

"If all we knew about Jesus were his walking habits, it would be significant. Jesus is a border walker. If you want to find him, you will find him walking along the borders. Borders are places where people either come together or split apart, join or divide. St. Paul, who knew — as we are trying to know — the spirit of Jesus, thought Jesus walked on three borders. 'There is neither Jew nor Greek, there is neither free or slave, there is neither male nor female, for you are all one in Jesus Christ.' The significant borders are ethnicity, domination, and gender. It is on those borders that splitting most often occurs. But when we reverse the gospel lament and have eyes that see and ears that hear, these dividing places can become meeting places. Communion can replace separation. Perhaps the story will show us the way this can be done? What are some of the borders you are presently walking on? Are they places of meeting or division?"

The people now talk. This will be the pattern for the evening. The leader will use the story to focus the areas of life that will receive sustained attention. The people will provide the actual stories and content within those areas. Each section of the story will end with an invitation to consider life in general and their life in particular from the point of view of the concerns of the story. The Jesus story and the stories of people's lives will be in dialogue.

When people first start to talk, it is one monologue after another, very little interaction. As the teaching continues, dialogue will break out. People will respond to one another. They will receive wisdom and support from one another. It is often difficult to surmise from the outside how this wisdom and support is being passed along. But once it happens to you, you realize there is a serendipity involved. It is unplanned and essentially unplannable. But after a while you expect that it will happen and you wait attentively. It never fails. The spirit moves through the story, the leader, and the community.

She continues.

> *Behold a Canaanite woman, living in those borders, coming forward, crying out, "Lord, Son of David, have mercy on me. My daughter is terribly troubled by a demon."*
> *He gave her no word of response.*

We are told to "behold" the Canaanite woman for she is the bearer of the revelation. Something is about to happen, and she is the catalyst of the event. Pay attention to her. She too is a border walker, and this is the story of a border walker meeting a border walker. Of the two border walkers we are not left in doubt about who is the most assertive. The woman is sketched as coming forward. If a confrontation is going to take place, she is going to initiate it. She is also noisy, crying out as she is coming forward. You can feel that something is about to happen.

She may be both assertive and noisy, but she is also insightful. She knows who Jesus is. She calls him "Lord, Son of David," a comprehensive set of titles. Jesus is Lord, and therefore meant for all people. But he is also Son of David, coming from a definite people with a particular heritage and distinctive traditions. Jesus is universal yet particular.

This is essentially the divine-human condition. Because we are related to God we are united to all that God sustains. Therefore, there is a universal quality to us. But we are also particular and concrete, a definite gender, a unique personality, and a member of a specific ethnic group. We are this one thing and not something else. It is this universal-particular paradox of each person that the Canaanite woman, who is the bearer of revelation, sees in an intensified way in Jesus.

The one who knows who he is also knows what he has to give. She asks for mercy. This is what the divine-human connection promotes. When the human is properly related to the divine, the divine — whose core is mercy — flows through the human. Since Jesus is the divine-human relationship in its most heightened form, she is only asking for the truth of him to come forth. What makes this begging for his truth poignant is her reason. She is walking still another border, the border of the sick and the well. Her daughter is in agony with a demon.

Although there may be many discussions about demon possession in the ancient world and how we might interpret these same symptoms today, one theological conviction remains constant. Demons twist creation in ways contrary to divine love. In one story the demons shout out from a possessed man, "We know who you are, Jesus of Nazareth. Have you come to destroy us?" Jesus' response is, *"Shut up! Get out!"* The answer to their question is, "Yes!" Jesus of Nazareth destroys demons because they attack God's beloved creatures. Can the demon slayer refuse his mission?

There is one last thing in beholding this Canaanite woman. She assumes that if Jesus has mercy on her, it will flow through her to her daughter: "Have mercy on me, my daughter is terribly troubled by a demon." She is in such solidarity with her daughter that any kindness shown to her will immediately enter her daughter. She is a conduit to her child. In other words, she not only participates in life, she is the flow of life into another. Is this not in finite form what God is in infinite energy?

In a few short lines Matthew has told us a lot about this woman. She has clear, unassailable knowledge of who Jesus is. He is the premier instance of the divine-human connection, meant for all yet coming from one. She knows what is supposed to happen from this intimate bonding of the divine and the human —

the flow of mercy. She knows the target of this mercy — wherever demons threaten God's good creation. And she wants this mercy to flow not for herself but for the one she loves. Without doubt this is Jesus' type of woman. Everything that she is about, he is about.

I wonder what it must feel like to be addressed like this? I wonder if we would easily accept it? It seems Jesus is having a problem.

He gave her no word of response.

However we might respond to it, it does not evoke a response in Jesus. This blunt description of his lack of response signifies a freeze-out. Jesus is refusing to recognize both her presence and request. This frosty silence forces the question "why?" Why does he not respond to this knowing, pleading woman who displays so many of the qualities he values? Why do we not respond to people who approach us in this way?

His disciples entreated him, "Get rid of her. She keeps shouting after us."
Jesus replied, "My mission is only to the lost sheep of the house of Israel."

The disciples, the storyteller's foil, are on hand to suggest a reason why Jesus is silent. Naturally, it will be the wrong one. As in so many gospel stories the narrative function of the disciples is to miss the point. Of course, they are portrayed as missing the point so that we might get it. The disciples think the woman is the problem. More specifically, they think the fact that she is making a scene is what is bothering Jesus. It is the eternal dilemma: crying women and embarrassed men. So, being experienced sycophants, they suggest to Jesus what they think he is thinking. In this way they hope they will ingratiate themselves and win favor.

However, they are wrong. The problem is not with the woman. Jesus' lack of response has nothing to do with her pleading and crying. There is nothing wrong with this woman. The problem lies elsewhere. It lies in Jesus' mind. He has construed his identity and mission not on the border but within the boundaries. He belongs to Israel and the gathering in of the strayed members of that house. This woman is outside that house, and so not of concern to the savior of the Jews.

It is important to remember that this identity of Jesus is a mental construction, not something built into the nature of things. It is true that Jesus is a particular never-to-be-repeated Jew, and every person who ever lived is a particular unique entity. The diversity of creation provides many different entities and so makes possible meeting and dividing. But it is the mind that turns the differences into separations, boundaries where "I" let off and "you" begin. The way Jesus has construed it, for the moment, is that he lets off where this woman begins. But not for long.

We often think the major problems are outside us. It is other people with their noisy demands that disturb our world. Have we ever taken the lead provided by this episode and looked at how we think about ourselves as central to our failure to respond?

She came forward and did him homage, saying "Help me, Lord."

She is reminiscent of other Gentiles in Matthew's gospel who knew who Christ was and did him homage: the Magi. But most important, she is not put off. Even Jesus' declaration of his exclusive Jewish identity and mission did not keep her from coming forward. When she addresses him, it is with a simple and unvarnished need. There is no flattery, no bargaining, no argumentation. Only pure vulnerability. "Help me, Lord."

In this plea there is a very important omission. When she addressed Jesus the first time, she called him, "Lord, Son of David." These titles acknowledged both his particular origins as a Jew and his universal outreach as Lord. Now she knows that he is stressing his Jewishness at the expense of his wider humanity. He is coming down on his particularity and slighting his universality. The result is that she is outside him and has no claim on his healing powers. In this situation she is certainly not going to remind him that he is a Jew. So she drops the title "Son of David," leaving only "Lord" to linger in his ears. Women with troubled children are remarkably resourceful.

When have we been reminded of our deeper identity? Has it ever happened when our narrower identity has been blocking the possibility of a creative response?

> *"It is not right," said Jesus, "to take the food that is meant for the children and throw it to the dogs."*
> *"Yes, Lord," she replied, "but even the dogs eat the scraps that fall from the master's table."*

This is a quick and remarkable bit of word play on the part of Jesus and the woman. Its dense symbolism is the key to the unblocking of the Son of David and the emergence of the Lord. I once read a scholarly article that reconstructed the roles of animals and in particular dogs in the time of Jesus. Dogs were not allowed in a Jewish house. In order to feed dogs with the "bread of the children," a Jew would have to take the bread off the table, walk to the door, open it, and throw it outside. The dogs were always outside the house. But in Gentile houses the dogs were allowed inside. If they wanted to feed the dogs with the "bread of the children," Gentiles did not have to go outside the house. All they had to do was reach down with the leftovers. The dogs were avidly waiting.

Jesus told the woman that in order to feed her he had to take the bread that was inside the house and throw it outside the house. She was an outsider and what he has belongs to the insiders. She says, "Yes, Lord." She agrees that the food belongs to the children or, in more theological language, salvation comes from the Jews. But she continues her emphasis on Jesus' universal outreach by calling him "Lord," the one meant for everyone. When Jesus lives within that identity, she is not outside the house. She is inside the house — perhaps not as a child at the table but as one who is eager for any food that Jesus has to offer. "I am already in the house, Lord," she effectively says, "just notice me."

In your experience how have outsiders become insiders? When has your identity expanded so that you were able to feed people who from an earlier and more constricted perspective were not part of your house?

"O woman," said Jesus, "great is your faith. Be it done for you as you desire."

The title "woman" that Jesus uses is not simply a description of her gender. And it is certainly a far cry from dog. I suspect that it means the one who gives life. And the one she gave life to is the one who calls her woman. I take the "O" to suggest a shock of recognition, a sudden revelation. The pestering one becomes the bearer of a deeper truth. This is her great faith. Through persistence and cleverness she reminded Jesus of his true identity. He is a Jew, but he is also Lord.

As a consequence of this powerful exercise of faith on her part, Jesus says something quite remarkable to her. Jesus is not usually swayed by the wishes of other people, either Pharisees or disciples. He is driven only by the will of his Father. That is his food and drink. In John's gospel he continually stresses that he does not do anything on his own. He says and does only what he hears from his Father. Therefore, it is remarkable to hear him say he will do the will of this woman. Could it be that in this woman's words he hears the voice of his Father? His Father's voice may come from the sky, but it also speaks from the earth, through the people who search for mercy in a demon-ridden world. Whenever and wherever Jesus hears his Father's voice, he is alert, ready, in touch, flowing. And that is what happened.

When have we heard words that stirred God's voice in us?

That very moment her daughter got better.

Once the block is removed, mercy flows freely. The flow of mercy was momentarily dammed by too narrow an identification. Once identity expands, mercy flows. So it is with us. Once we know our particularity is loved and cherished in the context of a wider universality and we shift the center of gravity from "I am this and not that" to "I am meant for all," mercy will not be a forced agenda or the imposition of an alien value but the simple expression of the deepest truth about us.

There was a recent incident in the news that made me think about the way mercy flows. At a court trial Lei Yuille, an African-American woman, explained why she and her brother helped Reginald Denny, the fallen white truck driver, during the April 1992 riots in Los Angeles. They were watching a television newscast "reporting live" and saw Reginald Denny being beaten. "My brother was in the room. He looked at me and said, 'We are Christians; we've got to help him out.' I said, 'Right.'" Then they got into their car and went to help the injured man.

Spiritual teachers stress that the flow of mercy is not the result of reasoned argument. It happens naturally when a deeper identity is realized. "We are Christians; we've got to help him out," leaves little room for rationalizing, calculating, or counting costs. Who they are overflows into what they do. When we are moved by mercy, it is often like that. We are moved, and the moving agent is a power deeper than mind, a power we call mercy.

We have all had that type of experience. Compassion stirs before we can think about it. There has been a spontaneous movement to include someone else. We have not pondered and argued and fussed. We have simply moved. This movement feels like a release of something that has been pent up inside us. At a later time we may be judged as foolish or reckless, but at this moment we are riding a spirit that, on a level deeper than rationality, is "right."

But we also know the opposite experience. We have "stood and watched." We are numb and indifferent to the plight of another human. Our feelings seem frozen. Our minds are manufacturing reasons for our numbness at warp speed. "It's not your concern. What can you do? They wouldn't help you. It's a shame but . . ." Then in a wonderfully perverse mental move, we may even count our blessings. "There but for the grace of God go I," we say. This pious egocentric remark is highly ironic. People truly in touch with God and grace would never utter it. It is the validation of separation, a blessing on non-productive pity and fearful distance. We have known the rushing river of compassion but also we are not strangers to the intricate workings of evasion.

What makes the difference? How is mercy released in us and how is mercy blocked? When is mercy a natural spontaneous act and when is it, if it is at all, a value which we have to remind ourselves we espouse?

The story of Jesus and the Canaanite woman suggests a spiritual dynamic that releases the power of compassion. Can this dynamic release compassion in us also?

This has been enough. Our minds now dwell within the mind of Christ. Persist in that dwelling.

※

This is how I imagine the Jesus stories might have been used by leadership within a community of people seeking spiritual wisdom, seeking guidance along the way of spiritual consciousness. Whether or not they were actually used this way, I do not know. What I do know is that I have used them this way. In classes, workshops, and retreats — with committed Christians, tepid Christians, non-believing people who were once Christians, and some non-Christians — I have slowly unraveled the Jesus stories. People have initially resisted this whole idea by saying that they no longer believe in this dogma or that ethical position that organized Christian religion proposes for belief. Or that religion is not for them. Or that they are too worldly and unworthy to participate in anything like a group using Jesus stories. Or they don't like Bible study groups. Or...

My response does not vary. "Do you suspect there may be more to reality than you are presently aware of? Do you ever get an inkling that there may be a spiritual dimension to yourself and the entire universe that is a key to who you are and what you do? If you do, this is one way to explore that hunch. Let these stories tell you what they know."

The Path Behind and the Path Ahead

To summarize: I first noticed my hesitancy to tell the Jesus stories straight. I could not tell them straight because there was too much there. I always wanted to explore the surplus. I was not capable of the admirable restraint of just telling the story as it was written and sitting down. But I also like to think I was honoring the stories both as literary forms and in continuity with their deeper intentionality. Just the way they are crafted demands slowness. Also the fact that they are laced with spiritual wisdom suggests patient and painstaking apprenticeship. Spiritual wisdom does not come easily to people attached to physical, psychological, and social ways of thinking and acting. We mistake it too quickly for what we already know and dismiss it.

I sensed "unsearchable riches" within the stories, and this made me uncomfortable with speed. It also made me uncomfortable with banality, with interpretations that were little better than common sense or, in many cases, a little worse than common sense. However, I could not do much better. The riches were there, but where was the key? Most obviously, it was with the people who spent the most time with the story. Enter the scholars and their gift of knowledge.

However, when I turned the last page of the book or underlined the summary conclusion of the article, I still sensed the "unsearchable riches" had not been searched out. More was needed. Exegesis had been performed, but full interpretation had not been ventured. The scholarship was like a surgery that did not contribute to healing. The stories sat there, their promises beckoning.

But how could they be realized?

By not trying so hard.

By being silent.

By going precisely to the place in the story that made no sense and dwelling there in acknowledged ignorance.

By recognizing that the story is more illumined than I am or ever will be.

By becoming willing, gradually and painfully, to die to some of my certainties so that there is enough emptiness in me for the truth of the story to enter.

By trying to change my attitudes and actions in the light of the spiritual wisdom and discovering cowardice and resistance.

By stopping the search for wisdom and beginning the prayer for courage.

By understanding that before you discover the heart you discover its hardness.

By acknowledging that what I was looking for on one level I was resisting on another level.

By sensing the moment of giving up was the moment of finding.

And the stories opened and so did I. The stories opened just enough to let me know there was more. I opened just enough to know adventure had returned.

So I began offering the stories. Although scholarship and theology were in the background, they were not in the foreground. It was just what I had found. I could not say it was the mind of Christ or the mind of the gospel writer or a sturdy staple of Christian faith. It was just what I found by living between the lines of the story. It was not the riches I tried to steal but the small wealth I was able to receive. If in hearing it there is worth, please...

So the path ahead is to offer Jesus stories to others.

Six offerings with reflections follow.

The first two, "The Sound of the Wind" and "The Voice from the Sky and the Struggles of the Earth," pursue the themes of finding, of coming in touch with the "you that is not yours and never can be."

The second two, "The Traveling Pallet" and "The Truth of Twice," explore selling, how disidentification, letting go, and dying are part of spiritual consciousness.

The third two, "The Secret of the Towel" and "The Road Less Traveled Is the Road Back," exemplify the struggles of buying, how we position ourselves in the eternal dynamics of receiving and giving.

Part 2

JESUS STORIES

FINDING

Chapter 3

The Sound of the Wind

JOHN 2:23–3:21

Now when Jesus was in Jerusalem at the Passover Feast,
many believed in his name when they saw the signs that he
did. But Jesus did not entrust himself to them because he
knew all things, and needed no one to bear witness to him
concerning human beings [tou anthropou], *for he knew what*
was in human beings [en to anthropo].

THIS SUMMARY DESCRIPTION of Jesus and his situation is the
introduction to the Nicodemus story (more about Nicodemus
in a moment). It sets the stage and highlights one of the major
themes of the narrative and theological reflection that follow.
Jesus is in Jerusalem at the Passover. He is in a sacred space at
a sacred time. The expectation is that there will be a revelation of
the sacred. However, in John's theology where there is revelation,
there is also rejection. The love of God always meets resistance.
It encounters both confusion and hardheartedness. And that is
exactly what is about to happen.

Jesus will reveal one of the essential conditions for understanding the revelation — the spiritual nature of the human being —
and it will not be understood. Nicodemus will prove a plodding
dialogue partner, unable to get unstuck from the mud. Then Jesus
will reveal the true nature of God — unconditional love for the
alienated world — and this revelation will provoke a division.
Some will walk toward the light, and some will walk away from

the light. Through it all Jesus will show that he knows what is in people, how they open to spirit and how they block it, what they resist and what they embrace.

On the surface the simple description — "many believed in his name when they saw the signs that he did" — seems positive. However, there is something lacking, for Jesus did not "entrust himself to them." Signs are manifestations of spiritual power in the material world. The proper response to signs is to trace the physical manifestations to their inner spiritual source. However, this is not occurring. People are fascinated by the signs, but they are not treating them as signs. They are marveling at what they see, gravitating toward the flashy, hungering for fireworks — and stopping there. They are scrambling to be around Jesus, for they believe in his power (name), but they are also succumbing to one of the perennial temptations of religions: miracle for its own sake.

This tendency of people to attach themselves to the surface of life frustrates the deeper drive of Jesus. He wants to give himself to people, to entrust himself to them. In order for this "handing over" to happen people cannot be stuck on the level of the physical. If all they can do is gawk at the signs, they will not have the inner receptivity to receive the One Who Comes Down from Above. In this story it is stressed that Jesus belongs to the world of spirit. If people want to receive that spirit, they have to recognize that they also belong to the world of spirit. The principle is: only "like" can know "like." If they would know Jesus as the One Sent by the Father, they themselves must have a relationship with the Father. "Jesus did not entrust himself to them." Not because he did not want to, but because he could not. The preconditions for him to indwell in them were not present.

What exactly does Jesus know about human beings?

People are capable of deeper spiritual communion and development, but this potential often goes unrealized. They settle for the surface. Miraculous power attracts them; spiritual participation eludes them. Jesus may see this clearly and need no one to bear him witness to this predicament. But the Johannine storyteller thinks that we need someone to bear us witness to this "stall" in responding to Jesus. Enter Nicodemus.

> *Now there was a human being* [anthropos] *of the Phar-*
> *isees, named Nicodemus, a ruler of the Jews. This human*
> *being came to Jesus by night and said to him, "Rabbi, we*
> *know that you are a teacher come from God, for no one can*
> *do these signs that you do unless God is with him."*

Nicodemus is quickly characterized. Although he is male, he is designated as a human being. The Greek word *anthropos* includes both male and female. Nicodemus is symbolic of a mindset that afflicts both genders. Also he is a Pharisee. "Pharisee" is gospel code for a mindset stuck on externals. Pharisees love first places at table, long robes with many tassels, salutations in the market-place, the bestowal of titles. They weigh the mint and the herb, but they neglect the weightier matters of justice and compassion. They are into the "passing show" of life. Lastly, Nicodemus is a ruler of the Jews and he speaks for more than himself. "We know," he casually and confidently remarks. This means he represents a perspective that is prevalent among the authorities. In typical gospel fashion little is written but much is insinuated. Nicodemus exhibits a point of view that besets male and female, that has difficulty getting beyond externals, and is prominently found among those who are leaders.

Nicodemus comes at night. His mind is in darkness. The upcoming conversation will show his obtuseness, his difficulty in following Jesus into a more illumined space. However, there is no conclusive ending to this episode. The dialogue between Nicodemus and Jesus slides into a theological reflection. Nicodemus does not exit; he fades away. He reappears two more times in the gospel of John, and scholars debate the role he plays in the entire gospel story. They are undecided about how to evaluate the overall portrait. Is he a creature of the night or is he moving tentatively toward the light?

My own "take" on this episode is that Nicodemus is not engulfed in darkness but stranded in twilight. He is not mesmerized by the signs. He realizes the signs point to something deeper: Jesus is a teacher sent from God. The signs in the material world bring him to look for a revelation from the spiritual world. He is at the next step. He wants a teaching, not another miracle. But before he can receive a teaching from God, he must receive a teaching about himself. This is where Nicodemus stalls.

> *Jesus answered him, "Amen, Amen I say to you, unless one is born from above/again* [anothen], *one cannot see the kingdom of God."*
> *Nicodemus said to him, "How can a man be born when he is old? Can he enter a second time into his mother's womb and be born?"*

That Jesus is a teacher sent from God is reinforced by his forceful mode of speech. He prefaces what he has to say with double "Amens." For ordinary people "Amen" comes at the end of sentences and signals the hope that God will hear the thought or petition. Jesus places "Amen" at the beginning of the sentence, signifying that God is already engaged and ratifies what is about to be said. Rhetorically, it means, "Wake up. Something important is about to be said." In this episode Jesus will use the double "Amens" three times. A foundational spiritual teaching is being revealed.

Nicodemus may want a spiritual teaching, but Jesus points to a block in his capacity to receive it. In an episode in Luke Jesus notices a similar block in the Pharisees who ask him when the kingdom of God will come, "You cannot observe the kingdom of God. Nor will they say, 'Behold, here!' or 'Behold, there!' For behold, the kingdom of God is within you" (Luke 17:20–22). Normal physical eyes, eyes that see objects and events, are not the type of eyes that see the kingdom of God. Eyes that come from a different birth are needed. If you are born from above — if you know yourself as spirit — then you are equipped to see the spiritual. Nicodemus called Jesus a teacher, and he is being taught.

The Greek word *anothen* can mean "from above" or "again." Nicodemus takes it to mean "again." He then pursues this line of thought to its ridiculous conclusion. Whenever I read his response, I see the headline of a sensationalistic supermarket tabloid: "Grown man returns to womb. Doctors stunned!" However, there may be a theological context that urges Nicodemus to his "off the wall" question. Physical birth from a Jewish mother is entry into the chosen people. Physical descent is not just a biological fact. It is also a theological privilege, a privilege that was clung to and used to claim superiority. In particular, it was relied upon in place of conversion. Why change when we are already chosen? This is the thrust of John the Baptist's bitter remark: "Do not presume to say, 'We have Abraham as our father'; for I tell you God is able from these stones to raise up children to Abraham" (Matt. 3:9). Nicodemus's physical persistence may be grounded in theological privilege.

Jesus will attempt to correct Nicodemus's misunderstanding.

> *Jesus answered, "Amen, Amen I say to you, unless one is born of water and the Spirit, one cannot enter the kingdom of God. That which is born of the flesh is flesh and that which is born of the Spirit is Spirit. Do not marvel that I said to you, 'You must be born from above [anothen].' The wind blows where it wills, and you hear the sound of it, but you do not know whence it comes or whither it goes. So it is with everyone who is born of the Spirit."*

New language is introduced, language geared toward bringing Nicodemus to understanding. When a woman's water breaks, the physical birth process begins. In this sense the human person is born of water. This is the necessary event of awakening into physical life. It is this event that Nicodemus has already focused on. But there is another birth that must build upon this first birth. This is a birth of the spirit, an awakening to the spiritual dimension of human life. This second birth refuses to reduce the human person to physical reality. Both births are necessary to enter the kingdom of God.

These two dimensions have corresponding capacities. One attunes us to the world of the flesh and the other attunes us to the world of the spirit. The full reality of the human person comprises both, but the emphasis is on spiritual capacity because the subject is spiritual, the kingdom of God. In another context St. Paul uses similar contrasts. "Just as we have been born in the image of the man of dust, we shall bear the image of the man of heaven. I tell you this, brothers and sisters, flesh and blood cannot inherit the kingdom of God" (1 Cor. 15:49–50). The entry requirement for the kingdom of God is spiritual consciousness, not physical consciousness.

Therefore, Nicodemus is not to marvel at being born *anothen.* It means "from above" and not "again." He is not to go "gaga" over what he mistakes as a weird physical proposal. Jesus is not about mystification. He wants Nicodemus to see, but to see with the eyes of the soul and not with the eyes of the flesh. He wants Nicodemus to awaken to the spirit in his flesh, and so he tells him what it is like. Imagery has provocative potential. Perhaps imagery can massage Nicodemus's mind and open it up to the deeper Mystery of who he is.

Being "born from above" is like the wind. It has it own intentionality. You cannot control or direct it according to your whims. It blows where it wills. You do not possess the wind; you ride it. Bird-like you stretch out your arms. Perhaps it will take you into the sky. You do not know where it comes from or where it is going. In contrast to the body that came from the womb and is going to the tomb, the origins and destiny of spirit are mysterious. But right now you are filled by the sound of it. It is the hum of being — present, vibrant, alive, now. You live by a spirit that is not you. Being born of this spirit is not an event "done and over." It is the "always-already-now" of life. It is the power of God living in you. Touch that ever so slightly in yourself and you will open to the teacher sent from God, and he will whisper things hidden since the foundation of world, the things he has heard from his Father, the things he is yearning to tell you. He will entrust himself to you.

Nicodemus said to him, "How can this be?"

Do I hear a groan from the reader or listener? Jesus may be a teacher sent from God, but he has met his match in Nicodemus. Nicodemus is not getting it. He mouths a series of frustrated "can" questions. When one is stuck on the level of the flesh, the affirmations of the Spirit appear as impossibilities. In spiritual teachings the principle is stated simply: the lower cannot understand the higher.

But perhaps as we watch Nicodemus grope about in the darkness, we are beginning to see the light. Could Nicodemus be a foil for our spiritual consciousness? We see him stuck and we become unstuck. Do not feel sorry for the literary character of Nicodemus. His ignorance is the path of our wisdom.

> *Jesus answered him, "Are you a teacher of Israel, and yet you do not understand this? Amen, Amen I say to you, we speak of what we know, and bear witness to what we have seen, but you do not receive our testimony. If I have told you earthly things and you do not believe, how can you believe if I tell you heavenly things?"*

The tone changes. Jesus is no longer teaching the truth of the Spirit. He is lamenting the conditions of the official teachers. Nicodemus began by recognizing that Jesus is a teacher sent from God. Now Jesus comments that Nicodemus is a teacher without understanding. This is just another statement of the ongoing gospel criticism that the people of Israel are not being properly taught. They are like "sheep without a shepherd." The problem is that the teachers do not have any personal knowledge of the Spirit. So they cannot understand the spiritual traditions they are meant to guard and communicate.

In contrast, Jesus, speaking in the plural for Christian teachers as earlier Nicodemus spoke in the plural representing the Jewish leaders, emphasizes, "We know." Personal experience of the spirit is the grounding of the Christian witness. "That which was from the beginning, which we have heard, which we have see with our eyes, which we have looked upon and touched with our hands, . . . we testify and proclaim to you" (1 John 1:1–3). Unfortunately, what is manifest and clear to one group because of their first-hand experience is darkness to another group. The testimony is not received.

The reasons why the Christian witness is not welcomed are many. This story focuses on a lack in the receivers, an ignorance in the ones who are listening. They do not have a sense that they are grounded in Spirit. These are the earthly things they cannot enter into: their own spiritual beings. If these earthly things are not grasped, how will they grasp the revelation from heaven? Jesus has struggled to show them they are "of the Spirit." He has been unsuccessful. The mind of Nicodemus will not open to the inner realm of the Spirit. Therefore, how can he possibly hear a revelation from the heavenly realm of the Spirit?

The teacher has been frustrated. He is not able to entrust himself to Nicodemus. But do not feel badly for Jesus. In the next chapter he will meet a woman at a well at noon, and she will drink in everything he is. But for the moment the storyteller will give the reader the revelation that has been denied Nicodemus. If Nicodemus is unable to receive it, perhaps the reader, who has been allowed to see the block in reception, will be open.

Now for heavenly things!

> *No one has ascended into heaven but he who descended from heaven, the Son of the Human. And as Moses lifted up the serpent in the wilderness, so must the Son of the Human be lifted up, that whoever believes in him may have eternal life.*

Do not trust those who sit upon the earth, with eyes shut, and travel into the heavens and then return to earth with knowledge needed for salvation. Beware of shamans. They will speak to you of things you do not know and demand that you believe them on the authority of their visions. In particular, they will tell you about judgments to come, about the measuring rod God uses for punishment and reward. Their knowledge plays upon your fear. Your not-knowing makes their knowing powerful. This path of revelation — ascending into heaven — is suspect.

No one goes into heaven except the One Who Comes Down from Heaven. It is not a matter of scaling the sky and peeking into heavenly secrets. It is a matter of understanding the true nature of Spirit. Spirit is not distant and so only accessible through otherworldly travel. Spirit enters into *this* world; we do not break into *its* world. It descends from above as the Son of the Human, not alien but intrinsically present, and its revelation is not about esoteric things and predictions of the future. The passion of the Son of the Human is to give life to all who are ready to receive it.

This imparting of eternal life will happen preeminently and paradoxically at the place where physical life is receding. The death of Jesus will bring life to his followers. This perception plays upon the ancient idea of sympathetic magic. This idea can be phrased succinctly: that which causes the suffering is that which relieves the suffering, only in another form. The text alludes to an example of this spiritual dynamic in the desert experience of Israel. The Israelites in the desert had questioned God's care for them. As a punishment, fiery snakes swarmed into their camp and bit many of them. They beseeched Moses, and Moses beseeched the Lord. The Lord told Moses, "Make a fiery serpent, and set it on a pole. The people who are bitten, when they see it, shall live" (Num. 21:8). So Moses made a bronze serpent and put it on a pole. When those who were bitten looked upon it, they lived. When what brought death was lifted up, it brought life. So it is with the Son of the Human. Death is the destroyer of people. However, when the Son of the Human dies, death will become the bringer of life.

Although this is the primary allusion of the serpent image, it also evokes other connections. The serpents in the camp bring to mind the serpent in the garden. The bite of that serpent broke the relationship of Adam and Eve with the Divine Source and brought death into the world. As the First Human Being brought death into the world the Second Human Being will bring life. But he will bring life precisely by dying. All are bitten by death. Yet when they look upon the One Who Has Come Down from Above in his death, eternal life will flow into them.

Besides this Genesis connection, there is the more general connotation that the snake sheds its skin and continues to live. This physiological fact became a symbol of the human person shedding the body and entering into a new life. In the rich symbol of the serpent on the pole the major thrust of the teaching is conveyed. The revelation is not esoteric knowledge about the future but a stunning communication of eternal life entering into our perishing flesh.

For God so loved the world that he gave his only Son, that whoever believes in him should not perish but have eternal life. For God sent the Son into the world, not to judge the world but that the world might be saved through him.

The reason for the imparting of eternal life is that God is love. It is the nature of God to love, and God is faithful to that nature. This love impels the Divine Source to send the Son, one who shares this nature and whose very essence is this sharing. Although the world is deeply connected to God, it is also deeply alienated. The Son has not been sent to condemn and thereby increase the alienation. The mission of the Son is to strengthen the connection and allow eternal life to flow into created yet alienated existence. In this way the nature of God as self-giving will be realized in the estranged world.

Many believe that these two sentences on the love of God and the mission of the Son are the essence of the good news. When we meditate on their positive implications, we may be overwhelmed. As many Christian mystics have attested, the love of God may flood into our hearts and bring about conversion and new life. However, equally stunning is what is denied in the divine makeup. It is not only that God is love but also that God has no interest in condemnation and perishing. This goes against both deep-seated instincts and explicit religious training. It is difficult to fathom that ultimate reality has no condemnatory side when all the proximate realities we deal with have judgment and condemnation as key features. Family, work, church, and state are quick to judge and condemn. If Nicodemus's obtuseness made him continuously ask, "How can this be?" our obtuseness is that we cannot take this revelation seriously. The One Who Came Down from Heaven revealed a God without vengeance. However, all those who scale up to heaven find a God settling scores, evening out the suffering, judging and condemning with glee. Judgment is essential to the moral life. How can it be missing in God?

If there is no judgment in God, how does judgment come about?

> *The ones who believe in him are not judged. The ones who do not believe are judged already. And this is the judgment: the light has come into the world and human beings loved the darkness rather than the light because their deeds were evil. For all who do evil hate the light, lest their deeds be exposed. But those who do what is true come to the light, that it may be clearly seen that their deeds have been wrought in God.*

Judgment is not a future event, but a present choice. It is self-judgment, the result of either responding or not responding to Jesus' revelation. It is not a matter of going before a Judge who weighs good and bad deeds and passes sentence. The atmosphere of trepidation and punishment associated with the law court is not the imagery of this text. More interior imagery is employed, imagery of "seeing and turning away" and "seeing and turning toward." This imagery leads us into a psychological and spiritual maze where attraction, movement, hesitancy, and refusal are intertwined.

What happens first is light. The light comes into the world, and the world and each of its inhabitants are suddenly seen in a new and penetrating way. We are connected and yet alienated from the Divine Source. This revelation becomes an invitation to either grow in connectedness or become more firmly entrenched in alienation. St. John's style is to paint contrasts. So naturally some move toward the light, and others move toward the darkness.

Those who move toward the light are already in touch with it to some degree. "For this was I born and for this did I come into the world, to bear witness to the truth. Everyone who is of the truth hears my voice" (John 18:37). This is the ultimate motive for Jesus' efforts with Nicodemus, to give him the first truth so that when the fullness of truth was spoken, he would "hear its voice." The ones gravitating toward the full revelation of the Divine Source already dimly surmise that the ultimate energy of their deeds is grounded in that source. Moving toward the light merely makes this more "clearly seen," brings greater consciousness of this truth. It is not that their deeds were totally wrought in God. I suspect that they, like all of us, are a mixture of light and darkness. It is rather that a deeper trust exists in them, an ability to put their ignorance and arrogance in the larger context of spirit and struggle. Therefore, they have more capacity to risk, to be drawn out of coldness to the warmth of the light. They sense the light is their true home and so they journey toward it.

The ones who love the darkness because they do evil are not unalloyed. The same that was said about those who come to the light can be said about those who stay hidden in the darkness. They are a mixture of good and evil. However, an identification with their sinfulness has developed within them. They do not know anything of Spirit within themselves so when the fullness of Spirit appears, it appears to them as judgment. The light is alien, a glaring harshness. Its only promise is that it will expose their mistakes and inadequacies. Therefore, they scheme to keep themselves covered — even from themselves. Lying to themselves and lying to others is the only strategy they can envision. They cling to this darkness out of fear. In this perverted sense they love it. It allows them not to be seen. Eventually they realize the only way to secure the darkness is to kill the advancing light. They think this will protect them, but it is proves to be their undoing.

In the strange and terrible providence of God this movement of violence on their part is still a movement. They come to the light to put it out. Only they do not know the light is a love that deeply desires their salvation. It wants to give them life. So it takes their violence into itself and returns love. And so out of human violence a sign is created, a sign that attracts the darkness in us, draws it out and then engulfs it. Divine love has strange and subtle ways. Its passion for human salvation cannot be stopped even by the human refusal to accept it. It is a light shining in the darkness, and the darkness is not able to overcome it. "When I am lifted up, I will draw all things to myself" (John 12:32).

A teaching about earthly things. A teaching about heavenly things. A teaching about heaven on earth.

A First Reflection: A Sound Called "No-Hit"

In Ray Bradbury's tightly told short story "Powerhouse," a husband and wife are riding their horses across the Arizona desert.* They are on the first step of a journey to see the woman's dying mother. The woman is trembling. She is unable to accept the fact that someone she loves will die.

Storm clouds are gathering and the couple is looking for shelter. They come upon a powerhouse of the Bureau of Electric Power. The building is humming with the sound of electricity. The sound seems to take possession of her. "The humming came up through her heels, into her medium-slim legs, and thence to her body. It moved to her heart and touched it. . . . Then it moved on to her head and the slenderest niches in the skull and set up a singing, as love songs and good books had done once upon a time. The humming was everywhere." The door to the powerhouse is open. To escape the impending storm they enter into the "solemn singing place."

The couple decide to spend the night, but neither can sleep. The woman muses on her husband. "His body held a faith like a maze, and the sorrow that struck into him was lost and gone before it finally reached where it wanted to hurt him." She asks why she never caught this faith from him. "It's not a catching thing," he says. "Someday you just relax. And there it is."

She tries to sleep, but suddenly the humming is in her and it is carrying her away. "The earth was suddenly more than many separate things . . . it all had one pattern encompassed and held by the pulsing electric web." The electric current enters her imagination and takes her from one home to another, from a death scene to a birth scene. She has a profound sense that she is not alone. "The singing went on higher and higher, and she was everywhere." She presses herself against her husband and cries freely.

In the morning her hands have stopped trembling. As they ride to see her dying mother, she asks her husband if sometime, perhaps on a Sunday, they could return to this place. He reckons so.

---

*Ray Bradbury, *Classic Stories 1* (New York: Bantam), 102–11.

"And as they rode on into town she was humming, humming a strange soft tune, and he glanced over and listened to it, and it was the sound you would expect to hear from sun-warmed railroad ties on a hot summer day when the air rises in a shimmer, flurried and whorling; a sound in one key, one pitch, rising a little, falling a little, humming, humming, but constant, peaceful, and wondrous to hear."

The humming of this story is the same as the sound of the wind in the story of Nicodemus. This sound is unlike other sounds. Physical sounds are caused by one object striking another. In Hindu literature there is a sound called "no-hit." It is not made by the clash of objects. It is the hum of being, the vibration of pure existence. It blows where it will because it is not produced by people. Also its origin and destiny cannot be traced, *but we hear the sound of it.* We know it because it is carrying us away.

Belonging to this spirit allows us to belong to everything. The woman in the story moves from being isolated and frightened to connected and peaceful. Her husband has the clue, "Relax. And it is there." Relaxing is the path of belonging, and paradoxically belonging is the path of transcendence. What we transcend is not the earth but our individual, isolated, and fearful existence. That is the sound of the wind. "So it is with everyone born of the Spirit."

A Second Reflection: The Spirit Is a Second Womb

I know a man who was born twice from the same woman. At first blush he would seem to be the man Nicodemus was looking for. However, in the final analysis, he is just a fortunate man who heard the sound of the wind in his mother's voice.

One day he was driving his mother to a funeral. She had been to many funerals — her husband's, her brother's, and those of most of her friends. She was out-surviving everyone she knew. But not without pain and grief. She had lost most of her money, suffered a heart attack, and had bouts of uncontrollable crying. This was not untroubled old age. As they drove along, she was calmly talking about her own wake and funeral. She had instructions to impart. She wanted it done according to her wishes.

Suddenly, she said, "I'm giving up on fear."

The man looked over at her. Their eyes locked. This was a deeper conversation than they were used to having. He returned to looking at the road.

"Everybody dies. Nothing is left. I'm giving up on fear." She said it as a matter of fact. No big deal. Just what was coming down.

"I've tried it," the man said. "It's not that easy."

What he really thought was that it is impossible. He had been haunted by fears — fear of sickness and death, fear of the future, fear of losing money and work. In one moment of insight he saw that fear completely structured his life, webbed him around, and was the principal motivator of almost every thought and action.

He looked across at his mother. She was beaming. He was incredulous.

They never talked about it again. But his mother began to change. She was never reticent to express her opinion, but now she spoke her mind on every topic. Yet without anger or righteousness or pomposity. This was not someone who was finally letting loose. Her words were wise and spoken directly from the heart. She showed an understanding and tolerance of human frailty that stopped people in the middle of harsh criticism. Her presence became something infinitely gentle and remarkably strong.

People wanted to be around her. Although they could not say what they took away, they left richer than when they arrived. Her son also came, not out of obligation but because she had become a fountain and he was a thirsty man. And slowly, it took a little more than nine months this time, she gave birth to his spirit. It was huddled and frightened deep in the darkness within him. It needed careful combinations of breathings and pushings to allow it to come forward. As long ago she had brought forth his body, so now she brought forth his spirit. He was born twice from the same woman.

I think this man is a brother to Jesus. Jesus would understand what is happening to him. Once a woman came up to Jesus and said, "Blessed is the womb that bore you and the breasts that nursed you!" Jesus spoke back, "Blessed is the one who hears the word of God and keeps it." This was not a correction, but a parallel truth. Mary gave birth to his body during nine months of blood sharing and finally birthing. As she interacted with him as he grew, she gave birth to his spirit, raised his consciousness above fear into the higher reaches of love. He was born twice of the same woman.

This is a gift. There is no controlling it. But if you are born of water *and* the Spirit through the same woman, there is a special wholeness to life. The harsh contrasts — what is born of the flesh is flesh and what is born of the Spirit is Spirit — are not needed. Flesh and Spirit are friends. Their commingling is complete. Therefore, the earthly prerequisite for the heavenly teaching has been met in a wonderfully integrated way. So when the heavenly teaching finally arrives and it reveals a divine love reaching out to a frightened world and a Spirit pouring itself into all flesh, the man born twice from the same woman smiles. He knows this teaching.

✳

Someone who read this little story commented, "Good for him. What about me?"

Unsolicited advice.

Hang around people who are Spirit-filled and releasing Spirit into the world — even your mother or father or brother or sister or son or daughter or father-in-law or mother-in-law or neighbor or co-worker. Spirit is contagious. It blows where it will. Get in the way of the wind.

Chapter 4

The Voice from the Sky and
the Struggles of the Earth

LUKE 3:21–4:30

SOME AMONG US rise higher. They say words and do deeds and people gather. They embody a truth that attracts. At first we gravitate to them because of these words and deeds. Eventually we want more. Although they are confronting forces in the outer world, we notice their undefeated energies come from the inner world. They are drawing from a well we cannot see. It is this well we yearn to drink from. We want access to their source. Where are they coming from? What experiences shaped them and who are the significant people in their lives? What is the path they traveled to get to the place they are at today?

If the person who attracts us is Jesus, we are fortunate. The gospel writers understand our spiritual hunger, our desire to apprentice ourselves to him. They write in order to reveal Jesus' inner reality, the source from which he comes, the passion that drives him. Once the well of Jesus is uncovered, we can drink from it. This is not done by stealth. We are not thieves in the night. Jesus' own self-understanding is that he came to give life and give it to the full. This life he gives is the very life that animates him. It is not something he possesses, but something that possesses him and through him becomes an offering to others.

So it is a match, a mutual desiring. If we are interested in where he is coming from, he is interested in telling us. If we are interested in drinking from his well, his cupped hands offer us the water. If we want to know his source, he is happy to make the introduction.

This question of the deepest identity of Jesus is symbolically phrased as, "Whose son is he?" and "Where does he come from?" The surface answers to these questions are "He is the son of Joseph and Mary" and "He comes from Nazareth." In the gospels these two responses reflect negative appreciations of Jesus. They are put-downs. "Is not this Joseph's son?" means, "Who does he think he is? We know the humble origins of this man and he should not pretend to rise above these." The phrase "Can any good come from Nazareth?" reflects the same prejudice. Nazareth is not known as the home of world-shakers. If this man comes from Nazareth, a high evaluation of him is misplaced. To know people's origins is to keep them in their place. It is a quick and easy strategy of dismissal to mention undistinguished parentage and small-village upbringing.

However, there is a gospel episode that is at pains to show that this appreciation of Jesus is too shallow. Staying at this level will not reveal the source of his startling words and deeds. We will not understand him or his mission. More importantly, we will not be able to share in his life. Our quest to join him in Spirit, to drink from his well, to participate in his Source will be frustrated. The story of the baptism, genealogy, temptations, and homecoming of Jesus in the gospel of Luke will open for us the truth we desire.

Baptism and Genealogy

> *Now it happened that when all the people were baptized and when Jesus also had been baptized and was praying, the heavens were opened and the Holy Spirit came down upon him in the bodily form of a dove. A voice came from heaven, "You are my beloved Son. In you is my pleasure."*

Jesus is baptized with all the people. It is a singular event in his life, but he is not alone. It is not an experience that makes him completely different from the other people in the water. He is participating in dynamics that affect "all the people." These dynamics concern a forgiveness of sin which entails a *metanoia*, a change of mind. Instead of "holding on to" all the wrongs that have been done to us and all the wrongs we have done to others, we let go. The sins are washed away in the waters of the Jordan. Sin is a reality in the life of "all the people." But we do not have to identify with that reality. This is the *metanoia,* the change of mind that is necessary, the mental release that is the prelude to new life. We have to quit defining ourselves as sinners. This is only a first step, but without it no other steps are possible.

When our sins drift away in the water, we have lost our identity. If we were strongly connected with sinful actions, their sudden disappearance leaves us empty. There is a moment when we do not know who we are anymore. We are between identities. Something has ended, but has anything begun? Jesus will show us the path *after* forgiveness. He was in the water with us. But now he is doing something "all the people" are not doing. Perhaps "all the people" can watch — and learn.

Jesus is praying. Prayer is the way we make ourselves accessible to the Divine Source. It is how we open to receive what the Divine Source is waiting to give. Prayer is not about petitioning a reluctant God to come across with the things we think we need. Prayer is a process of dismantling our protective devices so that we can adjust to the divine energies. What is often not appreciated is that our identification with sin is a protective device against God. When our mind clings to our sinfulness, we are not worthy. We dare not turn our face toward the Source of love, for it will surely judge us. Once sins are forgiven and the change of mind occurs, the emptiness that is created in our identity is an opening for God. Prayer is the natural next step after forgiveness.

The heavens open. The main thrust of the biblical imagination pictures the transcendence of the Divine Source in terms of the sky, "Our Father who art in heaven." Unfortunately, this heavenly imagery also connotes distance. The divine in the sky means the divine is not on the earth. People are cut off from God. For this distant God to come close the heavens have to open and a visitation has to occur. Something from the sky has to descend to earth. This something is the Holy Spirit. The very power and being of God arrives to Jesus who is praying. The transcendent God is immanently present. What was once distant because of sin becomes close when sin is forgiven.

The story says the heavens open. However, they only open because Jesus is open. In terms of spiritual psychology the heavens were always open. The Divine Source is always poised to give the Holy Spirit. As the adage has it, "The winds of God are always blowing. We must raise our sails." When we move through forgiveness to prayer, the sails are raised. What previously appeared closed now appears open. The truth is we are now ready to receive. God, as is God's wont, seizes the opportunity.

The Holy Spirit descends as a dove. This "bodily form" is a symbol that needs to be interpreted. The voice from the sky supplies the meaning of the dove. The dove carries a message of intimate love. "You are my beloved Son. In you is my pleasure." Jesus' ultimate identity is the receiver of divine love. This divine love is God's pleasure. It gives God pleasure to love people, to bring peace and reconciliation into their lives. At the birth of Jesus the angels sing, "Glory to God in the highest and peace on those who receive his pleasure." The new life of Jesus, his identity and mission, is to ground himself in the love of God and to cooperate with God's pleasure to bring this love to all people. From forgiveness to prayer to love to pleasure — this is the Christian path that is quickly traveled in this first scene of the story. It needs some underpinning. And nothing "underpins" better than a family tree, especially one that goes back to Adam and beyond.

Jesus was himself, beginning at about the age of thirty, being (as it was supposed) the son of Joseph . . .

Once Jesus knows who he is, he is "himself." A distinction that is often used in theological and spiritual literature is between the order of being and the order of knowing. To say that we are ourselves is to suggest that our knowing coincides with our being. The baptism and prayer experience of Jesus do not make him into something he was not. He is and has been the beloved Son and pleasure giver. The baptism and prayer event is a revelational experience. It tells him the truth of who he is. He comes into himself.

This deeper self is "beginning at about the age of thirty." All the work we do before we realize we are the beloved of God and the carrier of divine pleasure is preparatory. Spiritual identity —

knowing who we really are — is the beginning of spiritual work. Jesus now starts a work that is a co-work with God. This work engages the fullness of his human powers. This is symbolized by making Jesus the ideal age of peak capacity — thirty. He has a lesser identity, an identity that people mistake for the whole of him. Designating him the "son of Joseph" is inadequate to his reality. It is a "supposition" that cannot account for his fullness. But perhaps if we push through the genealogy a greater sense of completeness will emerge.

> ...*the son of Heli, the son of Matthat, the son of Levi, the son of Melchi, the son of Jannai, the son of Joseph, the son of Mattathias, the son of Amos, the son of Nahum, the son of Esli, the son of Naggai, the son of Maath, the son of Mattathias, the son of Semein, the son of Josech, the son of Joda, the son of Joanan, the son of Rhesa, the son of Zerubbabel, the son of Shealtiel, the son of Neri, the son of Melchi, the son of Addi, the son of Cosam, the son of Elmadam, the son of Er, the son of Joshua, the son of Eliezer, the son of Jorim, the son of Matthat, the son of Levi, the son of Simeon, the son of Judah, the son of Joseph, the son of Jonam, the son of Eliakim, the son of Melea, the son of Menna, the son of Mattatha, the son of Nathan, the son of David, the son of Jesse, the son of Obed, the son of Boaz, the son of Sala, the son of Nahshon, the son of Amminadab, the son of Admin, the son of Arni, the son of Hezron, the son of Perez, the son of Judah, the son of Jacob, the son of Isaac, the son of Abraham, the son of Terah, the son of Nahor, the son of Serug, the son of Reu, the son of Peleg, the son of Eber, the son of Shelah, the son of Cainan, the son of Arphaxad, the son of Shem, the son of Noah, the son of Lamech, the son of Methuselah, the son of Enoch, the son of Jared, the son of Mahalaleel, the son of Cainan, the son of Enos, the son of Seth, the son of Adam, the son of God.*

Genealogies are a bore to read, especially if it is someone else's lineage. For a storyteller genealogies are a challenge and can be a fun way of making some significant points. This genealogy, following the custom of the day, is made up completely of males. This lopsided and lengthy line-up is grist for the storyteller mill. For a while the storyteller may want to stress "son" until the omission of daughter becomes laughingly obvious. But as the list lingers on, the question of where it is going becomes more insistent. It is driving somewhere, but where?

Jesus is being traced back to the dawn of time and beyond. As this is happening, he is collecting all his ancestors and making them part of his identity. This is basically a remembrance of the people of Israel. However, near the end it breaks out of history into protohistory, and out of protohistory into eternity. Jesus is the son of Adam. He is the inheritor of all peoples and so the revelation of "all the people." Finally, he is the son of God, precisely what the word of the heavens said to him. Jesus is the revelation of the place where the divine and the human meet. And the divine and the human meet in every person.

But what does that mean?

Temptations

Jesus, full of the Holy Spirit, returned from the Jordan. He was led by the Spirit into the desert for forty days where he was tempted by the devil.

The Holy Spirit is now the energy of Jesus' life. He is filled with the Spirit, and the Spirit leads him into the desert to be tempted by the devil. At first this seems a strange activity for the Spirit. What about the petition "Lead us not into temptation"? Should not the Spirit be warning, "Look out for the devil. He goes about like a roaring lion seeking those whom he may devour"? However, in this story the Spirit seems to be arranging an introduction to the devil. What can be made of this?

The baptism and prayer experience of Jesus is a moment in time. The story does not say the heavens re-closed after they opened, but that is the usual way of things. The baptism-prayer is a special, revelatory moment. The problem with moments is that they are succeeded by other moments. A moment of ecstatic love may be followed by a moment of the loss of nerve which is then followed by a moment of mundane tasks. The spiritual path is not just recitals of ecstatic experiences. It entails the struggle to realize the insights of special times. What is heard in prayer must be allowed to restructure our sense of identity, reshape our desires, and redirect our emotions and actions. The truth of the spirit must be integrated into mind, body, and social relationships.

This ongoing process of realization happens when we test our new identity in action. In some translations of this passage it says the Spirit "drove" Jesus into the desert. I fantasize that the Spirit was in a hurry. It wanted to get the process of integration under way before the illumined state was forgotten or Jesus returned to the more mundane work of carpentry or, worse, Jesus went in search of other religious experiences. The real temptation is to treat the religious experience as a high to be continued. "It is good for us to be here," said St. Peter, experiencing the transfiguration of Jesus. "Let us build three tents." With this suggestion to try to make the vision permanent, the vision disappears. Basking in special experiences does not bring heaven to earth. It only creates more desire for heaven. When earth-bound people meet God, the next and quite appropriate encounter is with the devil.

The reason for this meeting with the devil is to clarify the identity of the beloved one. We become clearer about who we are when we refuse certain actions and endorse others. In the case of Jesus the devil will suggest attitudes and actions that are appropriate to the beloved Son of God. Jesus will see through these suggestions and refuse them. In his refusals he will come to understand more deeply the true meaning of the words he heard. "You are my beloved Son. In you is my pleasure."

In Christian history there has often been a difficulty in distinguishing God and the devil, the "good" spirit from the "evil" spirit. A tip. The devil uses conditional clauses, trying to twist things out of shape: "*If* you are the Son of God ... " God uses unconditional declaratives: "You *are* my beloved Son ... " Holding on to the unconditional in a world of conditions is the struggle that lies ahead for a hungry man.

And he ate nothing in those days. When they were ended, he was hungry. The devil said to him, "If you are the Son of God, command this stone to become bread."

Jesus answered, "It is written, 'Human beings shall not live by bread alone.' "

This is strange. The devil asks for a miracle which, in ordinary consciousness, would seem to be a perfect expression of Jesus' status as the beloved Son of God. Jesus refuses him. Instead, he refers to the scriptural wisdom that people cannot be reduced to their physical needs. Human beings need bread, but they cannot live by bread alone. In Matthew's version a key phrase is added: "but by every word that comes forth from the mouth of God." The word has already come forth from the mouth of God: "You are my beloved Son. In you is my pleasure." Somehow these words are more crucial than bread.

This first temptation alludes to another time in Hebrew history. The desert, the forty days, the stone, and the bread recall the exodus experience in general and one incident in particular. The people are grumbling that they are perishing from hunger. The Lord provides manna in the morning and quail in the evening. God gives food to his people. Then the people are thirsty. They complain. The Lord tells Moses to take his rod and strike the rock. Water flows from the rock and the people drink. The Lord has provided. But the panicky heart of the people has been revealed. The storyteller comments that the Israelites put the Lord to the test asking, "Is He with us or not?"

This Exodus incident can be read as a demand that God personally meet every physical need. When these needs are not met, people question whether the Lord is with them or not. Satan plays on this deep-rooted human way of testing. How can Jesus be the Son of God if he is hungry? Certainly what it means to be the Son of God is to be physically satisfied at every moment. If you are not, then you have to question if you are loved. However, in his life Jesus will be hungry (physically unfulfilled) many times. But he will not lose confidence in the fact that he is the beloved Son. Jesus will put together being empty and being loved. He will be able to realize the flourishing of the spiritual life in the midst of a withering physical life. He will not demand physical satiety as a sign of divine love. His words will not be, "Is the Lord with me or not?"

The first temptation has been passed. Jesus did not enter into the assumptive world of the devil. The way the devil thinks was not appropriated by Jesus. With this refusal a part of what it means to be the Son of God was clarified. However, this is a low-level temptation, a flirtation with physical deprivation. There are more subtle tests in the making.

> *And the devil took him up and showed him all the kingdoms of the world in a moment of time and said to him, "To you I will give all this power and glory. It has been given to me and I can give it to whomever I will. All of this will be yours if you worship me."*
>
> *Jesus answered, "It is written, 'You shall worship the Lord your God; Him alone shall you serve.'"*

Jesus may refuse miraculous sport, but the devil shows no such restraint. He takes Jesus up higher, presumably in mid-air, to get a better view of what is about to happen. But also "up" symbolizes that this temptation is on a higher level. The first interchange concerned the physical level of life. This duel will be fought on the social level. The kingdoms of this world are seen in a flash. From the devil's point of view this is quite a trick. From Jesus' point of view this is a lightning flash of perception. He sees them for what they are. Their secret foundations are revealed to him. He understands how they work. How they work is not how his Father works, and Jesus does the works of his Father.

These kingdoms of the world have been given to the devil. Therefore he can pass them along to whomever he pleases. The reason the devil owns these kingdoms is that they work by his power. His power is contained in his names. "Devil" (*diabolus*) means tearing apart, division. "Satan" (*satanas*) means accusation. The kingdoms of the world work by the power of accusation and division. If Jesus would own these worlds, he must own them on their terms, the terms of the one who would give them to him. He must enter into the world of accusation and division, learn its dynamics and excel at it. Worship means to take on the characteristics of what you worship. It is not neutral activity. The devil's offer is not without strings.

However, Jesus worships something else. His Father's way of being is not accusation and division but forgiveness and reconciliation. The power and the glory of the kingdom of God are radically opposed to the power and the glory of the kingdoms of the world. The devil's enticing false alternatives make that quite clear. The path of the true Son of God is appearing in contrast to the path of the false Son of God that the devil is mapping out.

In the first temptation Jesus elected to live in the tension of being loved and being hungry. Now he chooses the tension of being loved and being socially powerless. Of course, this foreshadows the course of his life. He will not have power on the terms of the kingdoms of the world. In fact, he will be rejected by those who do have that power. He will not play their game. This choice is the way of the cross, and anyone who makes it should have no illusions about where it leads.

Jesus has passed the second temptation. But there is a still higher place for the devil to take him, a place where the Son of God will certainly be at home.

> *He took him to Jerusalem and set him on the pinnacle of the temple. He said to him, "If you are the Son of God, throw yourself down from here. It is written, 'He will give his angels charge of you, to guard you,' and 'On their hands they will bear you up, lest you strike your foot against a stone.' "*
>
> *Jesus answered him, "It is said, 'You shall not tempt the Lord your God.' "*

Two characteristics of the devil become clear in this exchange. He likes miracles, and he can quote scripture. In the desert he suggested a transubstantiation of rock into bread. In the air he managed a "light and sound" show, conjuring up a vision of the kingdoms of the world. Now on the pinnacle of the temple he is suggesting a miraculous float. People often equate true religion with miracles. Here the antithesis of true religion traffics in miracles.

Also, in the first two temptations Jesus quoted scripture. Here Satan returns the volley. This results in the proverb, "Even the devil can quote scripture." It also underlines the fact, often forgotten, that quoting scripture is not as important as understanding the spiritual perceptions that ground it. It might be too facile to say that an implication of this story is to avoid people looking for miracles who quote scripture. The combination seems to be deadly.

Around the pinnacle of the temple are carved the wings of eagles. The eagle is an image of divine care. The mother eagle takes her young on her wings and flies high in the sky. Then she collapses her wings and the young eaglets flutter and fly. Some stay aloft and some begin to fall. The mother eagle flies under the ones who are struggling, catches them on her wings, brings them up higher, and the training begins again. She guards them and bears them up. They do not dash their foot upon a stone.

The image of the caring parent, even if the parent is from the animal world, is a staple of the religious imagination. The gospels use it regularly. The gospels also use the imagery of angels. They are emissaries of divine care and guidance. Satan is playing with both these images, but he is using them in such a way that Jesus has to reject them. Satan twists the love of the Father into meaning immunity from harm. In fact, Jesus can put himself in deliberately dangerous situations and expect to emerge unscathed. This is a powerful fantasy, and the devil is presenting it as the true meaning of the Son of God. Jesus refuses this fantasy for the same reason he has refused the first two temptations. To be the beloved one is not to be exempt from the negative experiences of life, but to realize that divine love is a perduring reality that is not dependent upon circumstances. Jesus will not be safe. In particular, he will not be safe in Jerusalem, but he will still be the beloved one. Satan cannot seduce him into equating love and safety.

When the devil had finished all his temptations, he went away from him until an opportune time.

Without a deep identity the choices of life are just a series of options. However, once we have an identity, we are immediately confronted by what it means and how it should be enacted. There is no shortage of suggestions and they all appear reasonable. A good case can be made for miraculous food, political power, and supernatural privilege. Yet they are all fantasies, projections of ego dominance. They betray the voice from the sky. They are not true manifestations of what it means to be the beloved.

Also temptations are never over. They await opportune times. In Jesus' life these temptations will return at the crucifixion. When he is on the cross, he is most vulnerable. He is paying the price for his rejection of the path of fullness, power, and privilege. The priests, the soldiers, and the "bad" thief repeat his titles: "*If* you are the Son of God...*If* you are the Messiah..." They echo Satan's use of the conditional clauses. He is the Son of God only *if* something happens. What will prove it to them is *if* he comes down off the cross. One last try, one final suggestion about what it means to be the Son of God.

Homecoming

At this point in the story we know what it does not mean to be the Son of God. But what does it mean?

And Jesus returned in the power of the Spirit into Galilee, and a report concerning him went out through all the surrounding country. And he taught in their synagogues, being glorified by all.

Jesus' rejection of false alternatives increased the power of the Spirit in him. He became "hot news." Rumors about him spread. He taught in the synagogues, and people loved it. This broadbrushed portrait is important for what is to follow. It is a setup for his homecoming, where he will also teach in the synagogue and people will be loud in his praise — until they fully grasp what he is saying. Then the hometown folks will realize he is not the returning son of Joseph they had hoped for. This will not be a happy discovery.

> *He came to Nazareth where he had been brought up. As was his custom, he went into the synagogue on the Sabbath. He stood up to read and there was given to him the scroll of the prophet Isaiah. He opened the book and found the place where it was written:*
>
>> *"The Spirit of the Lord is upon me,*
>> *because he has anointed me to preach good news to the*
>> *poor.*
>> *He has sent me to proclaim release to captives*
>> *and recovery of sight to the blind,*
>> *to set at liberty those who are oppressed,*
>> *to proclaim an acceptable year of the Lord."*
>
> *And he closed the book and gave it back to the attendant, and sat down.*
> *The eyes of all in the synagogue were fixed on him.*
> *He began to say to them, "Today this scripture has been fulfilled in your hearing."*

It can be argued that drama is not the strong point of gospel stories. However, dramatic effect is certainly part of the story-teller's intent in this episode. Careful detail leading up to the reading — stood up, received the scroll, searched and found the proper passage. The reading. Careful detail leading away from the reading — closing the book, giving it back, sitting, the beginning of his speaking. The eyes of all fixed on him. The punch line. Pay attention, the storyteller is saying, this is important.

Jesus uses the words of Isaiah to speak the truth about himself. This was not the reading of the day, a happy synchronicity. Jesus knew the passage and searched for it. He is steeped in the scriptures. He may have an ecstatic experience at prayer after his baptism, but how he interprets that experience is guided by the sacred scriptures of his people. He used scripture to keep his balance against the dizzying proposals of the devil. It helped him know who he was not. Now he consults scripture to express his positive sense of identity. Personal religious experience is most accurately interpreted in the context of tradition and community.

The section from Isaiah unfolds the second comment of the voice from the sky. The devil hammered away on what "Son of God" must entail. "In you is my pleasure" is the beginning of the true meaning of Son of God. God's pleasure is to liberate the human from all that oppresses it. The poor hear the good news, the captives are free, the blind see, liberty reigns, and it is a year to make all things new. "Son of God" is not a privilege but a mission. It is not a title of honor but a task in the world. To be a Son of God is to bear forth the divine pleasure. The divine pleasure is to set the human free and watch it flourish.

If you have ears to hear it, this is happening today in your hearing.

Part of the crazy wisdom of the Spirit is the way it ignores commonsense approaches to time. The Isaiah quotation envisions a much different state of affairs than presently exists. It is natural to think that it is something to be worked for. It is a future hope, not a present reality. However, Jesus' emphasis is on fulfillment today. As Paul says, "*Now* is the acceptable time" (2 Cor. 6:2). Waiting is over. Longing is no more. Yet, it is many years since all eyes were fixed on him and these words were spoken. Have the Isaiah prophecies come true? How are we to understand fulfillment in the "now," in the no-waiting "today" of this story?

Scholars often point out that Jesus is the kingdom in himself. In his personal life he receives his being and love from God and manifests that being and love to others. This one sanctified person opens the possibility of sanctification of all. This is available "now." There is no need to wait. Nothing has to be done. It is a matter of turning away from sin and opening to what is there. The phrase of the opened heavens — "You are my beloved Son. In you is my pleasure" — is spoken in every moment. It is a matter of hearing and believing. When that happens, there is a beginning. "Today this scripture is fulfilled *in your hearing*." There is the rub. "In your hearing" does not mean that Jesus spoke loud enough and they heard the words. It means that if you hear it and turn, everything is available. Nothing is missing. You have all you need.

However, they have ears to hear but do not hear. They have heard but they have heard on their own terms.

> *All spoke well of him and marveled at the words of grace that came out of his mouth.*
> *They said, "Is not this Joseph's son?"*
> *He said to them, "Doubtless you will quote me this proverb, 'Physician, heal yourself! Do here in your own country what we have heard you have done in Capernaum.'"*

The townspeople are pleased with what they have heard. But "marveling" is always a mixed response. It signifies that they are impressed, but it also connotes that they do not understand. Marveling can be the first step toward comprehension. But it can also be a stage at which people are stuck. In the case of the townspeople it means that they missed the full import of what Jesus was saying.

Their question, "Is not this Joseph's son?" is not a question. It is gleeful anticipation. They are rubbing their hands in delight. It is the perennial gesture of "good things coming," personal gain in the offing. Jesus has spoken of benefits, and since he is Joseph's son and a hometown boy, these benefits will surely come to them. If Jesus has struggled with privilege and rejected it, they presume it. It is this presumption that Jesus brings to the surface. It is also a presumption he is about to subvert.

> *He said, "Truly, I say to you, no prophet is acceptable in his own country. But in truth, I tell you, there were many widows in Israel in the day of Elijah, when the heavens were shut up three years and six months, when there came a great famine over the land. Elijah was sent to none of them, but only to Zarephath, in the land of Sidon, to a woman who was a widow. And there were many lepers in Israel in the time of the prophet Elisha. None of them were cleansed, but only Naaman the Syrian."*

The seriousness of what Jesus is about to say is prefaced by "truly" and "in truth." Prophesy is not about pleasing people. It is about speaking the truth that no one wants to hear, the truth that is covered up by the comfortable. Jesus revisits two of Israel's greatest prophets and remembers them precisely in their mission to the Gentile world. Their feeding and cleansing powers were given to non-Jews. The message is: the people of Israel should not assume privilege. People are elected for mission and not for their own prestige. It is only "supposed" that Jesus is the son of Joseph and meant for the small village of Nazareth. The real truth is that Jesus is the Son of God and meant for all people. This universalism that is central to Jesus' retrieval of the prophetic tradition is not well received.

> *When they heard these things, all in the synagogue were filled with wrath. They rose up and led him to the brow of the hill on which the city was built so as to throw him down. But he passed through the midst of them and went away.*

It is a short step from marveling to wrath. They may not understand the import of the Isaiah text, but they do not miss the fact that they may miss out. They are alert to self-interest and angry when it is frustrated. What happens next is a harbinger of the crucifixion and resurrection of Christ. They lead him out of the city built on a hill. Nazareth is a small town. The city built on a hill is Jerusalem, and the crucifixion of Jesus takes place outside the walls. However, the attempt to kill Jesus is unsuccessful. He walks through the midst of them and goes his way. The crucifixion will open into the resurrection. Physical force cannot stop spiritual power. The Son of God, the One who embodies divine pleasure, is still alive and walking the earth.

A First Reflection: Beginning Whenever

There is a great fascination with the hidden years of Jesus' life. What was he doing in Nazareth from the age of twelve to his inauguration at the age of thirty? Some people have him diligently at work at the carpenter's trade, probably at a neighboring Roman construction site. Others have him squirreled away in an Essene monastery, learning the esoteric knowledge of those who are awaiting the Messiah. Still others have him traveling to foreign lands. In particular, he journeys to India and encounters the wisdom and compassion of the Buddha. People want a preparation for the public life of Jesus that is flamboyant and esoteric. The sudden introduction of the baptism, genealogy, temptations, and homecoming seems too abrupt.

Speculation is fun.

What fascinates me is not the vacant period of Jesus' life, the time the evangelists have neglected to recount. If factual autobiographical data is important for understanding Jesus, the evangelists have failed on a large scale. Their lapses of memory include more than "the hidden years." However, it seems they were more at home with symbolic remarks than with hard facts. What is more intriguing than what they have left out historically is what they have chosen to include symbolically.

In particular, the simple remark that Jesus is beginning at the age of thirty carries a surplus of symbolic meaning. It does not represent a certain chronological age but a certain stage of consciousness. When he knows he is the beloved and when this knowledge so permeates him that he is in the fullness of his powers, he starts. This means that beginning is not solely a temporal marker. We may have albums celebrating times that are now gone — birth, kindergarten, high school, college, marriage, etc. Finally, on the tombstone our temporal existence will be bracketed by a beginning and an end. These truths of temporal passage must be honored. They are as blatant and as persuasive as anything in the physical world. Cemetery walks are nothing if not sobering.

However, the suggestion in the story is that Jesus begins when he realizes he is loved. This realization energizes him. Whatever he does, he does out of this identity as the loved one. This means that old work, work we have done for years, may suddenly "begin." Also relationships that have as long a history as the boring genealogy of Luke may suddenly, and perhaps for the first time, "begin." Not because they have not been there, but because the one who is there now is new.

A beloved filled with the pleasure of God is driving his car to work the same as he did yesterday. Only it is not yesterday. Although it is the same person, it is the same person with a different consciousness. Amen, Amen I say to you — he is *beginning* to drive. A beloved filled with the pleasure of God is pushing her child on the swing the same as she did yesterday. Although it is the same person, it is the same person with a different consciousness. Amen, Amen, I say to you — she is *beginning* to be a swing pusher. Could it be true that every time we realize we are the beloved filled with the pleasure of God, we begin? The world is new and so are we.

This is hard to believe. We are entrapped in time. We were once young, and now we are old. We were once newly married, and now we are veterans of the institution of matrimony. We were once starting our careers, and now they have peaked. Time does not lie and neither will it be mocked. Get real!

Eternity does not lie either. Neither will it be mocked. A seventy-eight-year-old man who realizes love and says it to the nurse who is turning him in bed begins. A woman who realizes love and refrains from criticizing her teenage daughter who sorely needs criticizing begins. No one doubts we are a temporal duration. Pile high a life of curses and blessings on the scale of time. But to view it once from the realization of the loved one filled with divine pleasure is to see a different reality. When everything is a beginning, every ending is bearable.

A Second Reflection: Carrying Home in Your Heart

Not long ago I returned to my childhood home. I stood in the gangway between the two-flat I grew up in and the two-flat next door. When I was small, this gangway was a canyon. Now my shoulders nearly brushed the bricks of the two buildings. I looked up. The walls of the buildings squeezed my sight. All I could see was a narrow, rectangular slice of sky.

Then I remembered.

One summer day when I was about seven, workers were tar-ring the roof. I was in the gangway, loitering around their ladder, staring at the strange, ugly, and foul-smelling tar machine and looking up at the tar bucket that hung over the side of the roof.

Some tar fell and hit me in the eye. My instincts were fast and I closed my eyes in time. But the tar burned and it caked and hardened over one eye. I couldn't see.

My mother took me upstairs and put hot cloths on my eyes. She carefully washed away the tar, gently stroking and pulling. Even-tually, the closed eye opened. I could see fine. I was thankful. To re-turn me to complete normalcy, my mother walked me to the corner coffee shop and watched me slurp down a chocolate milkshake.

Early Christians called Jesus eye-salve. He cured blindness. The title came from a story in the gospel of John called "The Man Born Blind." The man born blind was not one unseeing man, but the condition of every person. Jesus spits in the earth and makes a paste. He then rubs the paste on the man's eyes and sends him to wash in the pool of Siloam, which means "Sent." He washes and sees. The symbolic message is: the seeing are sent.

This is Jesus' message to his hometown folks. The prophesies of promise are meant for all. The election of the people of Israel is for mission. They are not to hate the Gentiles and band together against them. The destiny of Israel and the destiny of the rest of the world are closely connected. Jesus is rereading their history so that they may see and be sent.

However, they are blind. They are portrayed as suffering from the stereotypical myopia that is encountered by someone who "goes home to the village where he was reared." They are insular, turned in on themselves, unable to see a larger reality, and greedy for whatever benefits them. They live under a narrow, rectangular slice of sky and tar has fallen into their eyes.

When he arrives, they think he is the same old Jesus. But he has changed. He has descended into the water and then through prayer received the gift of the dove. He has been tested in the desert, in mid-air, and on the pinnacle of the temple. A young man left; a seasoned man returns. They welcome him for who he was. They try to kill him for who he has become.

There is a special poignancy to Jesus' initial reception and final expulsion from Nazareth. Did Jesus first hear the Isaiah passage in that very synagogue? As a small boy did many of the people now listening to his boldness nurture him with the stories of the prophets? If Jesus is like the rest of us, his upbringing planted seeds. Where he is now is indebted to where he has been. This is the community and tradition that have provided Jesus with the language and vision to explore his beloved status. To talk about himself he borrows from Isaiah.

Many people find themselves in similar positions. They say, "I have outgrown the narrowness I grew up with." This may be the case. But often a more subtle judgment is called for. The things that made for growth then are not the things that make for growth now. What now is seen as insularity was once the protective environment needed for nurture. Who you are now is not totally different from who you were then. One stage of development should not denigrate another. Most likely, you have carried more with you than you left behind. When Jesus walked through their midst and out of their village into his world, I am sure he took Isaiah with him.

The famous quote says, "You can't go home again." Sure you can. But you probably can't stay. In the worst of situations they will push you out. In the best of situations you will carry home in your heart. It will be the memory of your first eye-salve. Your mother will be washing the tar from your eye, and you will see, and seeing you will be sent.

Chapter 5

The Traveling Pallet

MARK 2:1–12

It was heard Jesus was in the house. Many were gathered there, so many there was no longer room for them, even at the door. He was speaking to them the word.

RUMOR... Word got around... Somebody said... Jesus is in the house. In the gospels "house" is often code for the church. The church is where Jesus is to be found. He is not universally available like the earth, sun, moon, and stars. He is a man in history and, as such, is available through those who knew him, preserved his memory, and, given the full Christian confession, live out of his resurrected presence. In today's world where Jesus is a cultural icon, people seek to appropriate his life and teachings without the mediation of the church. However, all the documents we have about Jesus are church writings. There are Markan, Matthean, Lukan, Johannine, and Pauline Christs. Rigorous attempts are made to strip away this church influence and leave only Jesus. The reasons for this enterprise are wide-ranging, and the portraits of Jesus that emerge are diverse. But as far as this story is concerned, "It was heard Jesus was in the house."

Obviously, many heard. In escalating phrases the storyteller paints the crowded house — many, so many no room, not even at the door. Earlier Peter had said, "Everyone is looking for you" (Mark 1:37). They seem to have found him. In Peter's mind this

117

is obviously a sign of success. And surely this tendency to see crowds as a sign of success is part of the apostolic succession. Every pastor since Peter has been pleased with high attendance. The first question of every worship service is, "How many?"

Packed.

Jammed to the rafters.

Spilling into the street.

Breaking the fire codes.

They couldn't get in the door.

Jesus is speaking to them the word. But we do not get to hear what Jesus is saying. There will be an interruption. Jesus the Speaker of Words will be replaced by Jesus the Engager of People. What we will see is what Jesus was speaking about. The story will show the teaching/preaching in action. The Word will have become flesh once again.

> *Four people came carrying a paralytic. When they could not get near to him because of the crowd, they removed the roof above him. When they had made an opening, they let down the pallet on which the paralytic lay.*

When scholars talk about narrative, they often mention that it reflects the unpredictability of life. The mind creates "logical sequences." It plots how things should happen, arranging events like flowers in a vase. Often "things" are compliant. They go along. Then the unforeseen happens. We scramble for a response and everything flows in a different direction. The arrival of the four bearers and the paralytic is not prepared for in the story. It is the unforeseen that changes everything.

However, their top-down entry has been anticipated. The crowded house that signaled the success of Jesus' ministry is now seen from another perspective. The people anxious to hear Jesus are blocking the entrance. They have come close, but now no one else can get close. Is this a critique of the church? Is the predicament of the church that while it has gathered to listen to Jesus, it is simultaneously blocking access to him? It should be clearing a path à la John the Baptist but it has created a huddle, rear ends to outsiders. In particular, the paralyzed are being blocked. This is especially unfortunate, for Jesus has a peculiar understanding of paralysis and a peculiar way of dealing with it.

It is hard to restrain the imagination from picturing the descent. Suddenly dust and debris fall from the ceiling. (I once asked a group what was the first question they thought of after hearing the story. A man answered, "Who is going to pay for the roof?" He was in insurance.) People scatter. Jesus looks up. Where there was only roof, the sky appears. Then coming down from the sky through the roof is a pallet. Four men are lowering it. When it comes down far enough, the paralyzed man can be seen. Are his eyes the only part of him still capable of movement? And then there are Jesus' eyes. The story will tell us what they see.

> *When Jesus saw their faith, he said to the paralytic, "Child, your sins are forgiven."*

When Jesus sees the bearers, he sees people of faith. Could it be that what comes down from above signifies the divine will? It is God's will that the paralyzed find Jesus. Even when people block the way, the divine will is not thwarted. It finds creative contributors who ingeniously gain access to the source of healing. These bearers are people of faith because they carry the paralyzed to a place of possibility, a place that God desires.

Jesus connects the bearers and paralytic by his sequence of actions. He *sees* their faith but he *talks* to the paralytic, tying them together through his sight and sound. What Jesus says to the paralytic is abrupt and unexpected. If the arrival of the paralyzed one was unforeseen, so is this sudden introduction of sin. All the story has provided is "paralyzed one on a pallet." Jesus' remark focuses on the forgiveness of sin. This is quite a leap and takes the story along a different line. There must be some connection between physical disability and spiritual alienation. The story line assumes it, but to explore it we must look outside the story.

One long-lasting rendition of sin and suffering is to see one as the cause of the other. Our moral wrongdoings result in our physical maladies. Some think this happens through the mediation of God. God knows our sins and afflicts us accordingly. This makes God a direct cause of human pain and is abhorrent to those who believe God is love. Others think that the way sin causes physical suffering is an intrinsic relationship; the contamination of the spiritual order naturally overflows and corrupts the physical order. There is no need to posit an intervening God. This idea plays into contemporary sensibilities that have reappreciated spirit-mind-body connections. Disruptions in the dimension of spirit have mental and physical repercussions. Correspondingly, disruptions in the physical dimension reverberate through the mental and spiritual realms. Influences run both ways.

Is it possible that Jesus is making visible the spiritual underpinnings of a physical disorder? By seeing paralysis and saying sin he is stressing the integrated effects of spiritual alienation. If this is the case, an immediate alarms sounds. The physical, mental, and spiritual dimensions may be interrelated, but they are also distinct and have their own inherent dynamics. If someone is physically disabled, the full causes are most likely found in the physical realm. Moving to spiritual and moral considerations as the causes of a physical condition is usually inappropriate. The better working supposition is that the body goes its own way, and when disability occurs, the person is "at the will of the body." The spiritual dimension is activated as we formulate a response to the finite failure of the flesh. Although spiritual malaise may erupt in the flesh, the more common path is a breakdown in the flesh opening a path to the spirit. Therefore, if we are to read the story as assuming sin causes physical paralysis, we must tread carefully.

Another path would be to appreciate the whole story as an artistic creation, symbolic from beginning to end. Its major concern is to explore the spiritual dimension of life and it is conveying that dimension in physical imagery. The crowded house is the self-enclosed church. The four friends who lower the pallet from above could be the four corners of the earth that obey the divine will. Everything conspires to get the paralyzed to Jesus, even though the church blocks the way. The effects of sin are paralysis of the whole person and the effects of forgiveness are rising and carrying the sign of your paralysis into a new home. Is this way of approaching the story stretching it? Of course.

How might we stretch it a little farther?

Jesus addresses the paralyzed one as "child." This does not mean he or she is a youngster. It is an acknowledgement of the "child of God" dimension. This is the aspect of the human being that Jesus usually centers on. What sin does is cripple the child of God in us. What is unable to walk is the human person who is made in the image and likeness of God. The human person who is a sinner, the one alienated from the Divine Source, is walking very well, perhaps even running. But the child of God is paralyzed, unable to "go its way." The focus of the story is the liberation of the child of God from its imprisonment.

How is it possible to understand this dynamic of "child of God paralysis"? In Christian theology original sin precedes personal sin. We are born into a sinful condition that actively elicits our cooperation. Our personal actions ratify and reinforce the original sin. In contemporary slang, we get messed over before we mess other people over. We are wounded before we wound. We are injured before we inflict injury. The ultimate victory of sin is that it turns the victim into a sinner. We do unto others as has been done unto us.

What is the inner logic of this process that turns the victim into a sinner? The wrong that has been done to us is not just one more experience. It does not fall into the category of "over and done with." It sticks. It becomes a significant feature of our consciousness or, in an even more insidious move, we repress it and it takes up residence in our unconscious where it covertly influences every aspect of our being. In short, we form a secret pact with it. It becomes a hidden identity. We *are* the wrong.

The first sign of this negative identification is that it stops the production of good deeds. We become the bad tree that Jesus claims cannot bear good fruit, the thistle that cannot bring forth a fig. Then the stopping of good deeds unfolds into the doing of bad deeds. The wronged one does wrong. In one way this scenario goes against a rational approach. It would seem to be common sense to avoid doing to others the pain that has been inflicted on us. However, the dark truth is that the abused become the abusers. The sinner in us grows strong. The child of God is still present but in a weakened condition.

Finally, the child of God is unable to walk. The classic expression of sin is to be "curved in on oneself." This is precisely what happens. The only way this paralysis can end is to cut the knot which we have tied to the sin that has been done to us and which through a strange and dark embrace we have made so central to our being. The forgiveness of sins is the liberation of the true self. It is the foremost strategy for renewal in a world of alienation. Jesus is about restoring people to their true functioning as children of God. Forgiveness of sins is the way he does it. This divine drive in Jesus will be sharpened by contrasting it with another way of thinking. Enter the scribes.

> *Now some of the scribes were sitting there, reasoning in their hearts, "Why does this man speak thus? This is blasphemy. Only God can forgive sins."*

The scribes are seated, the official position of teachers. They are described as "reasoning in their hearts." This is a double-edged description, neither edge favorable. The first edge has to do with the heart. In spiritual teaching the heart is a space deeper than the critical mind. It is not a space of reasoning, weighing, measuring, judging, arguing, and debating. It is a space of compassionate presence, of a knowing that is built on communion and not distanced observation. The scribes have filled the space of compassionate knowing with critical judgments. They have erected a law court in the land of love.

The second edge is simply that they do not talk. They have noticed something in the outer world, but their inner disapproval does not reach the outer world. Judgmentalism and negativity flourish when they are not tested in dialogue. This quick sketch of the scribes will be contrasted with the picture of Jesus who does not reason in his heart but immediately perceives, whose inner world is not a protected environment but a rush toward action.

Since they are seated teachers, it is only natural that their consternation is theological. Their theological frowning might be strung together in this way. "Sin is an offense against God. Therefore, only God can forgive sins. If someone who is not God attempts to forgive sins, that person is arrogating to himself the power of God. This usurping of God's right by someone who is not God constitutes blasphemy." The scribes are guarding the divine prerogative. Christians have often countered this charge by claiming that in their orthodox evaluation Jesus is God. Therefore, he has the right to forgive sins. However, this response short-circuits the deeper criticism that unfolds in the story. It accepts the position that Jesus is about to challenge.

Playing the "Jesus is God" card also presumes that the conflict is between believers and non-believers. However, it must be remembered that the scribes are in the house. Although they were a religious elite within Judaism, they also represent a certain mindset. The mindset is universal, and it is as much present in Christian gatherings as in Jewish gatherings. In a nutshell, scribes represent people who are completely preoccupied with the question of authority. That is the essence of their complaint. Jesus does not have the authority. The saying "If all you have is a hammer, everything is a nail" applies here. Their hammer is authority. No matter what is happening, all they see is the nail of "whether you have the right to do it." They think this obsession is grounded in a divine vigilance. God is constantly concerned about people infringing on his turf.

There may be another way of understanding what is happening.

> *Jesus, immediately knowing in his spirit what they thought inside themselves, said to them, "Why do you think these things in your heart?"*

It is dangerous to hang around Jesus. Even though you do not talk, he knows what you are thinking. There is no need to leap to a supernatural explanation for this ability. The story gives us the connection. Jesus is deeply in touch with his spirit. This attunement to his own spirit allows him access to the spirit of others. This access is not a matter of mental moves, a strategic reasoning. Jesus is not reading the clues. The storyteller stresses that it is immediate. It is a knowing along a path different from that of our usual plodding. It is how spirit discerns spirit, not how mind figures out mind. Although Jesus asks why they *think* these things, he asks why they think these things in their *hearts*. As Christian spirituality has always maintained, the heart of Christ compassionately resonates with all hearts, even those turned in on themselves—particularly those turned in on themselves.

The question of why they are thinking these things is important. It is not rhetorical, but probative, exposing the constructive and reconstructive powers of the mind. They are "putting things together" in one way. It is possible to put them together in another way. Knowing the role of the mind in framing "reality" is an important step in spiritual development. We do not mistake our current categories for the "way things are." We are open to alternate approaches. For the scribes this openness will be helpful, for Jesus is about to propose another way of seeing what is happening.

> *Which is easier to say to the paralytic, "Your sins are forgiven," or to say "Rise, take up your pallet, and walk?"*

This question focuses Jesus' way of seeing the situation. He is not concerned with divine honor and privilege. His obsession is not authority but human liberation. If sin alienates people from their child of God identity, then forgiveness restores it. Forgiveness of sins and "rising, carrying, and walking" are two sides of the same coin. The word "rise" indicates resurrected life, life back in touch with the Divine Source. The path back to this relationship is by cutting the knot we have tied to the wrongs done to us and wrongs we have done to others. Forgiveness of sins is the power to walk. The answer to "Which is easier...?" is that they are the same thing. Forgiveness of sins is the power to walk.

There is a second subtlety to Jesus' question. It has to do with the connection between saying and doing, a connection that permeates the story from the first moment that Jesus is interrupted by the four bearers and paralyzed man. The unspeaking scribes have objected to Jesus' speaking, "Why does this man *speak* thus?" Jesus' responds by recognizing their thoughts ("Why do you think these things in your hearts?") and then proceeds to consider his own speech; "Which is easier to *say*, 'Your sins are forgiven' or to *say*, 'Rise, take up your pallet, and walk.'" On the level of saying both are the same. Neither is easier. Neither is harder. They are both vocal sounds. But we are about to move from the world of speech to the world of action and, in doing so, learn the true nature of what the scribes are fixated on — authority.

> *"But that you may know that the Son of the Human has authority on earth to forgive sins," he said to the paralytic, "I say to you, rise, take up your pallet, and go home." He rose and immediately taking up his pallet he went out before them all.*

Earlier Jesus connected the four bearers to the paralytic by looking at one and talking to the other. Now he connects the scribes to the paralytic by first talking to one and then to the other. In this way the exiting paralytic becomes the walking witness to real authority. The Son of the Human is the Son of God engaging the renewal of the earth. The type of authority the Son of the Human exercises is not concerned about "who has the right." It is concerned about authoring new life, about freeing people from paralysis. And it is effective. It brings about real change. It is not words. It is Word Made Flesh.

Three times in this short story a phrase is repeated with some variation. It is obviously significant.

"Rise, take up your pallet, and walk."
"Rise, take up your pallet, and go home."
"He rose and immediately took up his pallet, and went out
    before them all."

The command to "rise" is appropriate. It correlates with death and signifies that Jesus sees forgiveness of sins as a form of rising from the dead. Although death usually refers to bodily demise, we lose life in many ways. Relationships die, creativity declines, productivity fades, finances are lost, zest for life disappears, a way of thinking is discarded, a habit is killed. We are continually in the processes of dying and rising. In the story sin has destroyed this man's ability to walk in the light, to do good deeds. His reemergence is a coming back from the dead. The strong command "Rise" echoes the shout of another time and another place: "Lazarus, come forth."

This once paralyzed person does not stay in the gathering of the church. Nor is he enjoined to leave all things and follow Jesus. He is told to go home. The purpose of the healing is for him to reengage his life. His relationships and work that have suffered from his paralysis can now be revitalized. Obediently he goes out before them all.

The most intriguing symbol is the pallet. It is prominently featured in the story. The storyteller could have had the man rise and go home singing psalms. But in place of the expected jubilation is the injunction to drag along the pallet.

Why?

Is it a sign of his healing? He has overcome that which paralyzed him. What he was carried in on he now walks out with. Or is it meant to be a reminder? The pallet is the sign of his paralysis. His continuing memory of what once was will keep him in the world of mercy and gratitude. He will not harden into self-righteousness because there, in his home, is the pallet of his paralysis.

Or is he meant to use it to carry others to the source of healing as he was carried? Personal healing is not personal privilege. His new life is a mission to bring new life to others. He must find others paralyzed by sin, put them on the pallet that was once his, and carry them as he once was carried to the Source of healing. Do not forget that the door will be blocked, but the roof will open.

All were amazed and glorified God, saying, "We never saw anything like this!"

This seems like a wonderful ending. People are glorifying God, and the recognition that God has been the ultimate player in what they have witnessed is an important discernment. However, there may be an edge to the storyteller's closing line. When people are amazed, it often means they are one step short of understanding. In the empty tomb episode in Mark the women enter the tomb and see a young man dressed in white and "they are amazed"

(Mark 16:5). They are immediately told, "Do not be amazed." Amazement can close down deeper spiritual penetration of what is happening. "We never saw anything like this" is a statement of newness and power. Also it may signal that they do not fully "get" it. What has happened is wondrous, but the spiritual dynamism that informed it has not been fully appreciated.

A First Reflection: No Wretches in the Kingdom of God

The man crept into the back of the church. Early Sunday Mass, 8:00 a.m., last row, aisle seat. Barely in, quickly out if need be.

It was his habit since the divorce. He was afraid not to go to Mass, and he was afraid to go to Mass. So he snuck in and out. It was not that he was well known in this parish. When people looked at him, they would not be thinking, "Poor Don, what a messy divorce!" But he was thinking it. It was how he saw himself. In his head he was guilty, a major failure at matrimony. And at a young age. It was hard to handle. No matter how much they talked about forgiveness there was very little room for failure in the Catholic Church. The last row, aisle seat was a perfect place. It was where he belonged.

The old priest was saying the Mass. He was soft spoken, but if you paid attention, he made you think. He preached on the text where Jesus says the kingdom of God is within you. He was gentle, insistent, quoting from a gospel Don had never heard of. "If the kingdom of God is in the sky, then the birds of the air will precede you into it. If the kingdom of God is in the sea, then the fishes of the sea will enter it before you. But if the kingdom of God is within you . . . " The homily ended.

As usual, Don did not go to communion.

After communion a woman soloist sang a haunting rendition of "Amazing Grace." Every "wretch that was saved" was moved.

Except one. Suddenly the old priest was on his feet and walking toward the congregation.

"I hate that song. I am not a wretch. You are not a wretch. The gospel is right. The kingdom of God is within you. The kingdom of God is within you."

Then the old priest began moving down the center aisle. "This is my recessional song," he shouted.

Then he began to point to people in pew after pew. "The kingdom of God is within you. The kingdom of God is within you. And you. And you."

"Oh, no!" thought Don, as the priest approached with his jabbing finger. "Oh, no!"

"And the kingdom of God is within you," said the old priest in voice that was now quiet, not from exhaustion, but from the intuition that the truth he was saying had nothing to do with loudness.

Last man, last row, aisle seat: "The kingdom of God is within you!"

Don tried but he could not stop the tears. After a while he even stopped trying. Everyone walked by him. Finally, he stood up, walked out, and went back to his home.

We tie knots to our failures so tight we can barely breathe. We know we have to untie those knots, but we do not know how. Sometimes we untie them slowly, patient as a sailor, knowing the sea waits once we loosen the rope.

Other times it is a swift blow that frees us. An unlikely Jesus comes out of nowhere and wields the words of freedom. An old priest finds us hiding with our guilt in the last row and breaks through our self-hatred. We are unparalyzed and on our feet, striding out of the place we crept into, knowing that forgiveness and walking are the same thing.

A Second Reflection: The Perfect Penance of the Pallet

After forgiveness comes penance. But it is difficult to find the right penance.

In the Catholic confessions of my youth the penances were piddling. "Three Our Fathers and three Hail Marys." Of course, the sins were also piddling. Or the penances could be cute. "Take your little sister to the show. Help your mother around the house." Although it was taught that penance was absolutely necessary, I never really "got" what it was all about.

God freely forgave. Of course, you had to be sorry to receive the forgiveness. This sorrow could be imperfect. You might dread the loss of heaven and the pains of hell, and this self-interest would catapult you into sorrow. Or the sorrow could be perfect. You grieved because you realized you had offended God who is all good and just. Both these motives were acceptable, and they seemed to cover the range of human intentions.

So how does penance fit in? And what is the right penance for the "wrong" sin?

This phrasing might make it sound like an incurably narrow Catholic concern, a piece of arcane Catholic trivia. Actually it is an attempt to focus a human situation that few of us avoid. How do we break loose from our guilt? I am afraid it is not quite as easy as believing in a forgiving God and being sorry.

In the movie *The Mission* the Robert De Niro character has killed his brother and made a living by capturing and selling Indians as slaves. He comes to a space of deep sorrow for what he has done and how he has lived. The priest assures him God is all merciful. He is forgiven. Only his problem is not with God, but with himself.

He devises a penance. He ties all his armor and weapons in a net. Then he heads for the Indian villages dragging the net through forests and rivers and finally up the steep cliffs of a mountain. The Indians see him coming. When they see his suffering and resolve, they accept his sorrow and forgive him. And then he forgives himself. He cries.

In Morris West's novel *The World Made of Glass,* the major female character has been sexually abused by her father as a young girl. This started her on a life of sexual excess and debauchery. She goes into psychoanalysis with Carl Jung. This provides some help, but it does not free her of her addictions. On the advice of an Italian nobleman she begins to work with prostitutes, helping them with their physical and emotional suffering. This work functions as a penance for the years of abusing her own sexuality. Through this work she finds some relief and consolation.

Even when we are assured of God's forgiveness, we have to find forgiveness within ourselves. It is not enough to say that the divine passion is for redemption, not punishment. How many times can we hear that God wants us to walk again? Nor is it enough to say that we want redemption for ourselves. *We* want to walk again. We must find enough mercy within ourselves to forgive ourselves. Assurances of divine mercy are the beginning of forgiveness. They are not the end.

The De Niro character knows what he has to do. The sexually addicted woman also finds a path of redemption. But why are these the right penances?

Some people think there is a calculus of suffering in the world. The exact degree that you have contributed to it is the degree you have to relieve it. The De Niro character dragged many unwilling Indians through those rivers, forests, and mountains. Now he drags himself. The sexually addicted woman bought and abused many prostitutes in her life. Now she must tend to the same type of wounds she once inflicted. The perfect penance is the perfect payback. In this way the debt is paid and I can forgive myself.

As important as this exercise in balancing the scales may be, I think a deeper dynamic may be at work.

I fantasize that the pallet is the path of penance for the once paralyzed man. He must take it not only to carry paralyzed people to Jesus. What is equally important is what will happen within his consciousness as he performs this service.

I predict that at the beginning he will be aggressive and judgmental, quick to chide and warn. Next he will perform his service with a certain numbness. Having seen it all, he will do what is necessary without reflecting on it. Finally, he will touch a space of mercy in himself, a space that the Spirit of mercy has opened. Then there will only be mercy. Since there is only mercy, he will find he has forgiven himself.

The perfect penance is the one that can bring us into the land of mercy with such completeness that it can include even ourselves.

Chapter 6

The Truth of Twice

JOHN 8:1–11

NOW WHEN CHILDREN ASK, and they will, if the glory of God ever left the land and the people, they are to be told this story.

The glory of God resided in the temple; the divine home was the Holy of Holies. But it was an uneasy residence. The people were rebellious, either breaking or avoiding the agreements of the covenant. As their infidelity grew, the divine glory grew increasingly uncomfortable. If there was no justice or compassion or care, if the widow and orphan were neglected, if the rich were obsessed with possessions and the poor were harshly treated, then the God whose original and abiding desire was to free slaves could no longer live among such unfeeling people. The divine glory was forced to leave.

The departure was not abrupt. It happened in stages; the divine glory left in leaps. First, it bounded from its home in the temple to the Mount of Olives. It paused there to survey once again the ruin of Israel, to gaze on the people whom God loved but who did not love God. Then, half in anger and half in grief, the divine glory sprang into the heavens. The land of Israel was now bereft of Spirit. Sin had exiled the divine glory into the sky.

Now when children ask, and they will, if the divine glory ever returned to the land and the people, tell them this story.

Each of them went to their own home, but Jesus went to the Mount of Olives. Early in the morning he came again into the temple.

Everyone went home. However, for Jesus to go home he must follow a prescribed path, a path that includes an overnight stay on the Mount of Olives. The reason for this strange itinerary is that Jesus is the bearer of the exiled divine glory. When the divine glory departed, it moved from the temple to the Mount of Olives to the sky. Now it is returning by the same path, only reversing the direction. Jesus is the One Who Comes Down from Above (the sky). He proceeds to the intermediary Mount of Olives, and then returns to his home in the temple. In this way the divine glory "comes again" into the temple. It is early in the morning. So it is a new day. We can expect a new relationship between divine glory and human sinfulness. In the past sin drove divine glory away. Who knows what will happen when they meet again?

> *All the people came to him, and he sat down and began to teach them.*

"All the people" could not gather in the temple area. So it is not helpful to picture a literal mob trying to get close to Jesus. But what is about to transpire is meant for all the people. The intended audience is not just disciples or an isolated seeker or the adversarial Pharisees or the hardened rulers. Every life is involved in the processes that are about to unfold. The human condition is about to be revealed. All people are implicated. Therefore, "all the people came to him."

Jesus is seated, the position of a teacher. He has begun his teaching. However, the storyteller does not allow us to hear the teaching. We are not directly treated to the wisdom of Christ. As so often in gospel stories, there will be an interruption. We will not hear Jesus talk; we will watch him engage people. Jesus is not portrayed as a speculative thinker. He is someone who puts together thought and action, who encounters people in an effort to change them.

This is consistent with the overall gospel portrait of Jesus. He is continuously presented as a teacher with a difference, a teacher who teaches with authority. He is not a teacher who loves his teaching. He is a teacher who loves his listeners, and his listeners are in varying stages of openness and resistance to the truth he seeks to impart. Therefore, he engages both their openness and the resistance in order to effect change. The storyteller captures this truth about Jesus by refusing him a solitary monologue. We will not hear the profound teaching of a lone voice. In its place there will be group dialogue, many voices interacting. We will watch people respond to Jesus' words. As so often happens in John's gospel, resistance and openness will develop side by side. Therefore, Jesus will be alternating between encouragement and confrontation. The teacher is about to be interrupted so the true power of his teaching can be seen.

> *The scribes and the Pharisees brought a woman who had been caught in adultery. They made her stand there in the middle of everyone.*

"Caught–brought–made to stand there." Verbs of power, control, dominance. In two short sentences the scribes and the Pharisees are characterized clearly. What they are about is finding people in sin and holding them there. In particular, the picture of the woman "made to stand in the middle of everyone" conveys this holding action. They have surrounded her, and they are staring at her. The stare is the special tool of the self-righteous. The stare fixates people, turns them into objects, tries to hold them in the mistake they have been caught in. The unflinching eyes of the stare attempt to stay the flow of time and the newness it always brings.

Holding people in sin is not the "special gift" of the scribes and the Pharisees. It is an all-too-common human procedure. In fact, it is so common it is taken for granted. We do not consciously choose to do it; we just mindlessly engage in it. It is both pervasive and unreflected on. We just assume the obituary of a lawyer who died at eighty-two will prominently feature the scandal he was involved in when he was thirty-five. We unreflectively remark that she is doing well for an ex-addict, thereby using addiction as the permanent reference point for her life. Jail sentences are never over. We look at the fifty-year-old and see the twenty-two-year-old behind bars. Sin sticks. Ask anyone who has been caught, brought, and made to stand there.

Perhaps that is why the resurrected Christ in John's gospel brings the "glue of sin" to the attention of his disciples. He is trying to bring into their awareness an active and alienating habit. The resurrected Christ breathes on them and says, "Receive the Holy Spirit. If you hold people's sins, then they are held. If you let them go, then they are released" (John 20:23). This is the condition that characterizes our communal life. We can hold each other in our mistakes or let each other go. We can be a prison to one another or the source of release. Both are possibilities. But it seems we easily gravitate toward "holding in sin" and have to work at letting go. Perhaps this is part of what John means when he says, "They loved the darkness."

> *"Teacher," they said, "this woman has been caught in the very act of committing adultery. Now in the law Moses said to stone such women. What do you say?" They said this to test him, that they might have charges to bring against him.*

If they are nothing else, the scribes and the Pharisees are predictable. They have caught the woman, and they are holding her in her sin. But they have no sin to hold Jesus in. So they devise a trap to catch Jesus in sin. Then they will hold him in the sin they have trapped him into. The scribes and the Pharisees hold people in sin for a living. They are single-minded in this pursuit. Jesus is their target.

But their deceitful question has unwittingly given Jesus the raw material of his response. In the imagination of Jesus, the mystic-prophet, Moses/stones/the-very-act-of-adultery stirs up the founding events of Israel. Jesus is about to reenact them — with his own peculiar spin.

> *Jesus bent down and wrote with his finger on the earth.*
> *When they kept on questioning him, he stood up and said, "Let the sinless one among you be the first to cast a stone at her."*
> *And again, bending down, he wrote on the earth.*

Almost everyone at one time or another has given in to curiosity and asked, "What did he write?"

However, it is not important what he wrote. What is important is he wrote with his finger, he wrote on the earth, and he wrote twice. It is also important that he bent down, straightened up, and bent down again. These actions bring us back to the law of Moses and provide the answer to the question of the scribes and the Pharisees, "Now what do you say?"

In the Book of Exodus God writes the ten commandments and gives the two stone tablets to Moses. We are assured of divine authorship because we are told they were written with "the finger of God" (Exod. 31:18). Human authors use quills and parchment. God uses his finger, which is capable of carving into the hardness of rock. Jesus also writes with his finger, showing his closeness to God and that he writes for God.

When Moses descends from his mountain encounter with God, he carries the stone tablets to the people. As he draws close, he hears noise coming from the camp. Joshua thinks it is the noise of warfare. Moses correctly surmises it is the noise of revelry. He catches the people in the very act of committing adultery, of worshiping the golden calf. For the theologically minded prophets marital infidelity was always a metaphor for covenant infidelity. As a woman runs after another man (ah, patriarchal bias!), so Israel runs after another god. At the sight of this idolatry/adultery Moses throws down the tablets and breaks them. He stones the people with the stone tablets of the law. The scribes and the Pharisees know this story well. They also catch the woman (the people of Israel) in the "very act of committing adultery." They remember Moses' reaction. They also remember a law grounded in this type of fierce judgment. "In the law Moses told us to stone such women."

However, the story in Exodus continues. It is this continuation that the scribes and the Pharisees have forgotten. Moses returns to the mountain, pleads for the people, and in a long conversation with God suddenly asks to see God's glory. God accedes to Moses' wish but with a strange condition. "While my glory passes by I will put you in a cleft of the rock, and I will cover you with my hand until I have passed by, then I will take away my hand, and you shall see my back. But my face shall not be seen" (Exod.

33:22–23). The glory of God is overwhelming. A face-to-face encounter would mean death for Moses. Then the Lord tells Moses
to cut two more tablets. "I will write on the tablets the words that
were on the former tablets which *you* broke." The emphasis is on
the fact that it was Moses who did the breaking.

So God writes a second time. But between the first and the second writing the glory of God passes by Moses. When it does, it
has something to say.

> "The Lord, the Lord,
> a God merciful and gracious,
> slow to anger,
> and abounding in steadfast love and faithfulness,
> keeping steadfast love for the thousandth generation,
> forgiving iniquity and transgression and sin,
> yet by no means clearing the guilty,
> but visiting the iniquity of the parents
> upon the children
> and the children's children,
> to the third and fourth generation." (Exod. 34:6–8)

The divine glory, too great to look on directly, is steadfast love
and endless forgiveness. Yet this does not keep iniquity from being
passed on from generation to generation. The way of the earth is
the forgiveness of God meeting the entrenched iniquity of people,
the releasing God pleading with the holding people.

"Now what do *you* say?"

Here then is what Jesus has to say. It is not a proper understanding of the Mosaic law to stone people with the stone tablets.
The God who wrote the law is not punishing and vindictive. The
true interpretation of the Mosaic law is that God always writes
twice. And between the first and second writing is the reason why
two writings are always needed. There are no sinless ones. No
one can cast the first stone. Holding people in their sins while
holding yourself innocent is delusionary. The question is not condemnation but the continuing blindness of people to the universal
necessity of forgiveness.

There is an alternative to the holding stare of the scribes and the Pharisees. Jesus will exemplify it. He bends down, stands up with words that hold up a mirror to the scribes and the Pharisees, and then he bends down again. He does not stare. He does not hold them. He shows them their hidden sinful selves and returns to the earth. This self-knowledge is what is needed for them to change. The divine glory does not have to return to the sky. It has found another way to deal with the sinfulness of the earth.

Jesus writes with his finger: the sign of God's authorship. He writes twice: the sign of God's forgiveness. He writes on the earth: the sign of a universal condition. He does not stare at them: the refusal to hold them in their sin.

Are they able to read these subtle signs? Are they able to hear this complex blend of criticism and invitation?

When they heard this, they went away, one by one, beginning with the eldest.

"When they heard this" does not mean that Jesus spoke loud enough. It means they "got it." It penetrated into their minds and hearts. This offer of a different self-understanding — not righteous and vengeful but sinful and forgiven, not judge of this woman but the brother to her straying, not mouthing the words of the Mosaic law but faithful to its true meaning — became a clear invitation.

They refused it. They walked away. No reasons are given. In a way none are needed. Are there any on earth who have not seen themselves in a way that contradicted their cherished and scrubbed-up image and not looked away? We know how hard it is to look, especially when to look means to join with people we have previously despised. However, to refuse the invitation to community is to live in isolation. We walk away "one by one," alone and unconnected. Also the longer we have lived the life of self-righteousness and condemnation, the more difficult it is to see the truth and life-giving potential of an alternative. So it is the oldest who begin the procession of refusal, who turn away from the latest offer of divine glory.

That left Jesus alone with the woman in the middle. Standing up, he said to her, "Woman, where are they? Has no one condemned you?"

Earlier "they made her stand there." Now there is just the simple fact of mutual presence — no force, no "caught–brought–made to stand." Jesus stands up to look at her without staring, to show her to herself. In a gentle and non-holding way Jesus showed the scribes and the Pharisees a distorted self they did not know and yet needed to know in order to turn and have life. The scribes and the Pharisees had to see distortion before they could embrace life. This woman needs to see life before she can leave distortion. So Jesus shows her a deeper self that has always been present but now needs to be seen and believed. He calls her "Woman." This is not a simple designation that she is female. In the gospel of John the Mother of Jesus is called "Woman" twice, once at the wedding feast of Cana and once at the cross. "Woman" is a title of honor, pointing to a deep life-giving power.

Augustine said about this scene, "Only two are left — mercy and misery!" However, was Jesus ever satisfied with only two? Did he not want all people — "All the people came to him"? "Where did they go" is not a rhetorical or ironic question. Neither is it cynically gloating over a victory in a theological jousting match. It is a poignant question that I fantasize comes out of a hidden grief. Its impact is to cause us to scrutinize again the mystery of turning away from the offer of salvation.

The woman cannot answer the question of where the ones who refused the offer went. Nicodemus came at night and left in the same darkness. Judas walked away into the night. Did the scribes and the Pharisees also walk away into the darkness of not-understanding, into the night of endless self-deception?

Perhaps not.

Although they might not have been able to drop the stones, they could not throw them either. Perhaps they are in that troubled space between identities, the space where a life of hardness and judgment brings us all, a space where Jesus' next question to the woman presses us for an answer. "Has no one condemned you?"

"No one, Lord," she said.

For a story that traditionally has been titled "The Woman Caught in Adultery" it is significant she has only one line. But it is an important line. There is no condemnation in the outer world. The circle of accusers has dispersed. It has often been re-marked that there is a personal, deeper resonance to "no one." She does not condemn herself. For at least a brief moment the human judgmental world is nowhere to be found. What will life be without it?

"Neither do I condemn you. Go, and from now on no longer sin."

She calls Jesus, "Lord." So she knows he represents the Divine Source. His refusal to condemn means that there is no condemnation in God. We are now invited into a world of change without condemnation. All judgment in this world is in the service of hope. Everything is geared toward the unfolding of new life. We must all "Go!" Is there not an echo of God's ancient desire spoken through the mouth of Moses to whatever enslaves us, "Let my people go!"? With what we now know from this carefully crafted story, are we able to heed its final command? Can we walk without sin?

The divine glory has returned. Sin will not drive it back into the sky. It has written the "truth of twice" upon the earth and a new temple of forgiveness has been built in the precincts of the old. The divine glory is back home.

A First Reflection: Freeze Frame Forever

A friend of mine is fond of quoting a line from the play *Steel Magnolias:* "If you can't say anything good about anybody, you just come right over here and sit right next to me." Holding people in their mistakes is a popular pastime. Few can resist it. Even fewer understand the "handcuffing of people" that is really going on.

I have caught myself many times holding other people in their sin. But the strength and compulsiveness of this habit came home to me a number of years ago.

I found a man who had tried to commit suicide — pills and booze. I called an ambulance. They pumped his stomach and got him to the hospital on time. The attempt was unsuccessful.

However, every time I saw him after that, I saw him through the memory image of his attempted suicide. I could not shake it. I knew I was holding him in his sin, paralyzing him in his worst moment. Yet I could not let go. I wish I had a nice moral for this tale, but I do not. Although not many people knew of his attempted suicide, he moved away.

How does this "holding in sin" work?

It is quite simple and yet not easily grasped. I know something you have done. It is a wrongful action. It can be placed somewhere on the continuum beginning with indiscretion and ending with outright evil. But no matter where it fits on the continuum of wrongdoing, it has lodged squarely in my mind. It has become a permanent mental perspective. Whenever I see you, I see you through the lens of this mistake. I am holding you in your sin because the sin is the filter through which I approach and relate to you. To me you are always the guy with a DUI or the teenager who had an abortion or the cheat who did eighteen months for tax evasion, etc. I cannot let go of your sin, and, therefore, I hold you in it.

People whose mistakes are well known and therefore are "held in sin" by large numbers of people often leave for other communities or countries. People cannot or will not let go of their sin so they seek the company of people who do not know of their sin. These new people are not more virtuous than the people they are fleeing. It is only that they do not know the sin. You cannot hold what you do not know. We hide our sins because we know that if they are not hidden, they will be held. Skeletons are kept in the closet because we know other people will hang them on the porch. Then the only access to our house will be through the dead bones of our mistakes.

Negative gossip is great fun. It relieves boredom and makes you feel that no matter how bad you have it, you are better than that pathetic mess you have placed under the microscope. Holding people in sin is the perfect accompaniment to lunch.

Until it is you who are held.

A Second Reflection: The Path to Not Throwing Stones

Joining the human race is not as easy as it looks. Most of us do it only under duress.

Christian theologians often outline a triple solidarity to the human condition. We are united in creation, in sin, and in redemption. We are all created; we are all afflicted with sin; we are all in the process of redemption. However, we can opt out of any one of these solidarities at any given time. We can refuse the consciousness of dependence that characterizes creation. We can refuse the consciousness of alienation that characterizes sin. We can refuse the consciousness of conversion that characterizes redemption. If we refuse any one of these solidarities, we are on the path to isolation.

These three solidarities and our refusal to enter into them are tightly interlocked. If we do not admit dependence, we glorify ourselves, making our own ego the center of the universe. This dislodges the divine from its rightful place and immediately introduces us to alienation. Therefore, if we are to re-find our true selves, we must convert. The three solidarities — creation, sin, and redemption — play on one another.

However, if I had to pick one that really rankles, it would be solidarity in sin. After only a brief scan of time and history I can reluctantly admit to not being the whole thing and acknowledge dependence. Also I have always thought there was something dramatic, even romantic, about conversion. It feels adventuresome to come right out and say unrepentantly, "I am in the throes of conversion." However, it is solidarity in sin that really bugs my Pharisaical soul.

Flannery O'Connor's short story "Everything That Rises Must Converge" is an in-depth portrait of self-righteousness that must face its own sinfulness. The whole human world, a world that includes alienation, is beckoning Julian to join it. As the story begins, he has definitely refused the invitation. But by the story's end he will not be able to walk away. He will not be able to manage the escape of the Pharisees. He will get, as the pun says, his "karmuppance."

Julian is continually at odds with his mother, blames her for his own lack of success, ridicules her at every turn, and is always trying to get her to see herself as he sees her — ignorant, outrageous, and out of touch. The story has a startling twist that reverses Julian's plans. What he wanted for his mother he gets for himself. He is forced to look into a mirror and see his own insensitivity and cruelty. He tries to run from it, but the last line of the story predicts his future. "The tide of darkness seemed to sweep him back to her, postponing from moment to moment his entry into the world of guilt and sorrow." When we first have to acknowledge our sinfulness, the world of guilt and sorrow seems to be the only world there is. What the story of the Pharisees, the woman, and Jesus reveals is that it is the antechamber to another world, a world of mercy.

However, the world of mercy is a difficult place to dwell. Not because we do not think it exists but because we do not think we belong there. It is a place for other people. We enter it only when we cannot avoid it. Once there we look around at our new neighbors. They are not who we would pick. We are in real pain about our fall from perfection. Of course, we were never perfect. We were always sinful. All that is new is now we have faced up to it. In *A Man for All Seasons* the betrayer of Thomas More says, "I've lost my innocence." Cromwell replies, "You lost it some time ago. You've only now just noticed." It is the noticing that hurts.

However reluctant and painful our admission of sinfulness is, it begins a process. The next time we come upon failure, we quickly bend over and grab a stone. But we find we cannot throw it. It drops from our hand. Then another sin comes by. We reach again for the stone and again we cannot throw it. Finally, we bend down only to write on the earth — once before we stand to tell the truth of our solidarity with one another and once afterward.

Chapter 7

The Secret of the Towel

JOHN 13:1–17

I HAVE ALWAYS HAD A FONDNESS for the chapter headings of nineteenth-century novels. In my memory they read something like: "Lady Margaret swoons on hearing the news from Lord Jeffery's manservant that her dowry has been lost at sea. Alas to pirates!" The chapter that follows unravels these events in great and often nauseating detail. The chapter title is a summary of things to come.

The opening sentence of the footwashing scene in the gospel of John functions the same way:

> *Now before the feast of the Passover, when Jesus knew that his hour had come to depart the world and go to the Father, having loved his own who were in the world, he loved them to the end. During supper, when the devil had already put it into the heart of Judas Iscariot, Simon's son, to betray him...*

This beginning takes its time, leisurely layering thought upon thought, placing perceptions side by side without explicitly stating how they interlock. The words thread through the labyrinth of Jesus' consciousness and then suddenly jump to Judas and the devil who is eating slices of his heart. It is a summary of what is to come, a succinct statement that should not be forgotten as the action unfolds.

It is before the Passover, but this future celebration of the di-

143

vine act of human liberation has a present impact. It generates in Jesus a knowledge of his own exodus. It is not merely that he foresees his impending death. In fact, although death is hinted at, it is never explicitly mentioned. To put it flippantly, he is looking forward to a trip. Jesus is not a modern desperate hero haunted by termination. He is anticipating transition. There is a *"from"* and a *"to"* in his plans. He is departing *"from"* the world and going *"to"* the Father.

However, the ones he loves are in the world he is leaving. On the surface his exodus separates him from his own. He will be in one dimension called "Father" and they will be in another dimension called "world." In his present state Jesus has bridged these two dimensions. As John repeatedly states, Jesus has come from the Father into the world. This did not entail abandoning the Father for the world. Rather Jesus' presence in the world is simultaneously the presence of his Father. Therefore, he enables others to commune with the Father through him. Although the language might give the impression that Jesus travels from one dimension to the other, the truth is that he brings the two together.

Perhaps another bridge is being constructed by his leaving the world and going to the Father. It is not either-or but both-and. As the Father was in the world when Jesus was in the world, now the world will be in the Father when Jesus is in the Father. The Passover of Jesus is not an escape into a promised land, not the leaving of slavery for freedom. It is the bringing together of what was formerly alienated, the indwelling in one another of what was formerly separate. The reconciliation that Jesus effected constitutes a new state of affairs. It is a permanent opening of God into the world and the world into God.

Also this upcoming "hour" of Jesus is not his individual destiny, a fate reserved for him alone. It is the way in which he loves his own "unto the end." "Unto the end" are enigmatic words, resonating at many different levels. At least part of their meaning is that they point to Jesus' death. But they go further than the romantic notion that Jesus loved them "with and up to his last breath." In John's gospel Jesus' death is a completion, a way of fully communicating divine life to the human world. Later Jesus will say, "No one has greater love than this, to lay down one's life for one's friends" (John 15:13). For the Johannine Jesus dying is the path of loving.

Wherever love binds people together, loss is at first feared and then ultimately questioned. Is it as final as it looks? Loving and leaving may not be as incompatible as they first appear. On the surface death breaks relationships, but in the depths death is swallowed up by love. Jesus' love establishes a permanent connection, a connection that cannot be broken by physical separation. He has found a way to place leaving within loving so that departure is not an ending. The only reality that is "unto the end" is love. Everything else passes away.

However, this side of death and physical separation love often encounters another obstacle. Whenever we love and give ourselves, there is always the possibility of betrayal. Love is a reaching out that makes us vulnerable. We have offered ourselves and consequently have left ourselves unprotected. We expose ourselves so thoroughly only with our intimates, with those whom we care about, with "our own," with those whom we eat with. It is during supper that we are ripe for betrayal. A Judas lies in wait for every Jesus.

> *...Jesus knowing the Father had given all things into his hands and knowing he had come forth from God and was going to God...*

But Jesus' mind is not on Judas. It is where it always is; and the storyteller, often silent about the interior of Jesus, reveals the "heaven in his head." We are now in a position to grasp the whole of the upcoming episode: the inner, invisible world that energizes a deliberate action in the outer, visible world. This peek at the mind of Christ is privileged and important. John emphasizes the interlocking dynamics of knowing and doing. "If you know these things, blessed are you if you do them" (John 13:17). Now the first half is given. We are allowed entry into the self-knowing of Jesus. This is not one more piece of knowledge, something that he is conscious of. This is the structure of his consciousness itself, his basic framework of awareness, the permeating context of everything he perceives and does. This is what he always knows as he knows other things.

And what an all-encompassing consciousness it is!

He is aware of where he has come from and where he is going. He knows his whither and his whence, his origin and his destiny. This is God-consciousness. But it is not just the awareness of infinite Mystery, of the twin darknesses on either side of individual human existence. This mystery has the name of "Father." It is a generating love that creates, sustains, and transforms all things. This generating love has given "all things" over into the hands of Jesus. This is the "all things" of "through him all things were made" (John 1:3) and "he told me all the things I ever did" (John 4:29). In other words, Jesus will reveal the truth of this generating love to "all things." Therefore, what will follow will be a key moment of revelation. The eternal God will be shown forth in time and space. Naturally, there will be some restriction. The infinite will appear through the finite. But there will also be illumination. And when the content of the revelation is perceived there will be consternation. Expectations will not be met.

> ... *rose from supper,*
> *laid aside his garments,*
> *and girded himself with a towel.*
> *Then he poured water into a basin*
> *and began to wash his disciples' feet*
> *and to wipe them with the towel with which he was girded.*

In general, we do not find elaborate details in gospel stories. One exception is the Good Samaritan story in Luke. As the Samaritan descends into the ditch, we watch his every move. "He went to him and bound up his wounds, pouring on oil and wine. Then he set him on his own beast, brought him to an inn, and took care of him. The next day he took out two denarii and gave them to the innkeeper, saying, 'Take care of him. Whatever more you spend, I will repay you when I come back'" (Luke 10:34–35). This careful unfolding of detail carries its own message. Love means hands-on, time-consuming, and expensive work.

In a similar way John provides a world of detail. This detail is even more striking because it is in the context of God-consciousness. The story moves from the inner, "infinite" awareness of Jesus' consciousness to the outer, finite care of feet. From the highest to the lowest, so to speak. We watch the Word becoming flesh, not in one miraculous leap but in stages. It is a picture of descent, and the storyteller allows us the appropriate time to assimilate it.

Jesus rises from the supper and lays aside his garments. In his rising Jesus is distinguishing himself from his disciples. Later in the story he will resume his place at table and put back on his garments. At that point he will be one of them. But at this moment, given the reaches of his consciousness, he is acting in the name of God and he is "other" than they are. He is revealing the truth of the Infinite One. This is symbolized by laying aside his garments. We will now see the naked truth. Nothing will be hidden.

What will we see? What is the secret under his outer garments?

Under the outer garments of the One who has come from God and is going to God and to whom God has given everything is a towel.

He girds himself with a towel. He is preparing to work. This scandalous scene suggests God is a servant. And scandal of scandals, this divine servant works on the Sabbath. When Jesus healed the paralyzed man, people were angry because he cured him on the Sabbath. He replied, "My Father is working still, and I am working" (John 5:17). Later he reflects, "Amen, Amen I say to you, the Son can do nothing of his own accord, but only what he sees the Father doing. Whatever the Father does, the Son does likewise" (John 5:19). When the outer is stripped away, the inner truth is seen. It is a man girded with a towel, preparing for a certain type of work, a work he sees his Father doing, the Father who has handed "all things" over into his hands.

Jesus pours water into a basin and washes and dries the feet of his disciples. This is a symbolic action that evokes multiple meanings. Feet symbolize the journey of life, walking in time and over space. Inevitably they become battered and bruised, carrying the marks of struggle. They need to be cleaned and refreshed. The water purifies and soothes. And Jesus not only washes the feet, he dries them. They are ready again. The journey now can be continued. And the One who performs this servant activity is none other than God.

This is startling. It is not how people conventionally think of God. It is a far cry from a sign in the sky. There is no display of cosmic power. If this is a revelation of the *mysterium tremendum et fascinans* (the tremendous and fascinating mystery), it is not overwhelming but underwhelming. Most of all it is confusing. So it is time for that wonderful foil of confusion and misunderstanding to make his appearance.

> *He came to Simon Peter, and Peter said to him, "Lord, do you wash my feet?"*
> *Jesus answered him, "What I am doing you do not know now, but afterward you will understand."*

Peter's confusion has to do with who should be washing whose feet. In Peter's mind it is inappropriate for the Lord to be engaged in this task. It should be reversed. Peter should be washing the feet of Jesus. After all, Jesus is the Lord and Peter should be serving him. This is certainly the conventional mindset of superior-inferior relationships. God is a king and people are the subjects. The rules of the relationship are clear. Subjects serve lords. In this mindset the Lord serving Peter makes no sense. Therefore, Peter resists receiving the ministrations of Jesus. In theological language, he refuses to open to the free gift of divine grace.

Jesus states the obvious. In terms of the spiritual dynamics of knowing and doing, Peter does not know. Therefore, he cannot discern the meaning of the action. It does not fit his present categories and so he flounders. However, there will come a time ("afterward") when Peter will understand. Scholars often suggest that "afterward" means after the crucifixion and resurrection. When the whole story is known, each part will become comprehensible. This is undoubtedly true, but it is a long time to wait. And within this story Jesus asks them, "Do you understand what I have done for you?" There may be a quicker path to comprehension.

"Afterward" may mean after the footwashing. Peter may have to let Jesus wash his feet even though he does not understand. The preferred sequence may be knowing and doing, but there are times, many times, when doing precedes knowing. After Peter has the experience, he will come to understanding. Risking an experience that confuses him in his present mindset may precipitate a cognitive breakthrough. As spiritual traditions have often intimated, the way to understanding is through submission. As Peter looks down at the Lord carefully caring for his feet, something may shift in him. The foundation of a tightly held hierarchical view of life may crack. He may glimpse the new world that Jesus is inaugurating. Then again he may not. The decision to undergo a certain experience is always a gamble. It is a gamble that Peter is unwilling to take.

> *"You will never wash my feet," Peter said.*
> *"If I do not wash you, you have no part with me,"*
> *answered Jesus.*

Peter is adamant. His God-image has completely imprisoned him. God is a separate, self-sufficient reality that is meant to be worshiped from afar. The God who flows like water into the life of wearied people is beyond his imagination. Peter cannot negotiate the movement from a distant king to a humble servant. His refusal is a testimony to how powerful God-images are. Once they are espoused, they are capable of alienating us from the true Divine Source.

Jesus does not meet the problem head on. He does not argue with Peter's mindset. He restates his own revelation. He washes feet. That is what he does. He cannot do everything. He cannot be whatever Peter wants him to be, a creation of Peter's God fantasies. He only does what he sees his Father doing. If Peter cannot accept the flow of divine love from Jesus, he and Jesus will have to part. The only way to stay close to Jesus is to let him wash you.

Jesus' words could be read as a threat. If Peter does not go along with the footwashing, he does not go along "period." However, I believe it is more a statement of a simple fact. And as a statement of simple fact it moves the conversation into the area of personal allegiance. It is geared to move Peter out of his mind and into his heart. Peter loves Jesus, but he does not always understand Jesus. His love will not let him walk away. "Where will we go," he says at one point. "You have the words of eternal life" (John 6:67). Peter does not always understand these words, but he intuits that Jesus is the path to the Father. That is enough to keep him close. Jesus' words trigger this deeper level of love. Peter responds with the words of love. Extravagant words, if not downright overkill:

> *Simon Peter said to him, "Lord, not only my feet but also my hands and head!"*
>
> *Jesus said to him, "He who has bathed does not need to wash. He is clean all over. You are clean, but not all of you."*
>
> *For he knew who was to betray him, that was why he said, "You are not all clean."*

Peter's remark is a revelation of his character. He is impulsive yet not fully comprehending. He is so committed to Jesus that if Jesus insists on washing his feet as a condition of staying close to him, he will go the extra mile and request a complete bath. This shows generosity, loyalty, enthusiasm, and even good humor. However, it does not show understanding. In one sense, Peter has moved from resistance to compliance in the course of the conversation. In another sense, he is still without understanding.

Jesus corrects Peter's understanding without dampening his ardor. Peter's words reveal that he is thinking about a physical washing. However, Jesus' physical washing is symbolic of a spiritual renewal. God is Spirit and the first focus of divine attention is the human spirit. "If you have bathed, you are already clean" is a statement of the physical order. In that way all the disciples are clean, for they have all bathed.

However, the phrase "not all are clean" ironically twists the physical appraisal into the spiritual world. The "not all are clean" signifies betrayal, and betrayal is not a matter of skin but of the inner spiritual center. In the introduction the storyteller said Satan had entered into the "heart" of Judas. The interior is the target of Christ, and so it is the interior where betrayal must occur. Later, when Jesus dips the morsel and gives it to Judas, the storyteller will comment that Satan entered him. The food of Christ may be what Judas is physically swallowing, but it is a spiritual counter-power that is possessing him. The physical level is not the primary arena of struggle. The soul is where the action is.

> *When he had washed their feet, and put back on his gar-*
> *ments, and resumed his place, he said to them, "Do you*
> *know what I have done to you? You call me teacher and*
> *Lord. You are right, for so I am."*

The revelation of divine love is over. The washing has happened. The sign has been given. Now Jesus reverses the dynamics of revelation (rising from table and taking off his garments) and returns to concealment (putting on his garments and resuming his place at table). When he rose and stripped, we were privileged to see the transcendent love of God. Now this special time is over. Jesus is covered and back at table. The aftermath of revelation is usually puzzlement. What does it mean? What does it imply? Are there other towels under other garments?

Jesus asks these further questions. Earlier he had firmly stated that Peter did not understand the dynamics of knowing and doing associated with the footwashing. Now he phrases it as a question to all of them. But before they can answer, he compliments them on their complete grasp of who he is. They call him "Lord" for he is in union with the Father and so capable of revealing divine reality. That has happened in the act of footwashing. He is also "Teacher," the one who explains what the revelation means. That he is about to do. The Teacher is in the traditional position — seated and robed. Can the teaching be far behind?

> *"If I, then, your Lord and Teacher, have washed your feet,*
> *you ought to wash one another's feet. For I have given you*
> *an example, that you also should do as I have done to you.*
> *Amen, Amen I say to you, a servant is not greater than his*
> *master; nor are the ones who are sent greater than the ones*
> *who send them. If you know these things, blessed are you if*
> *you do them."*

A straightforward "take" on this teaching would interpret it as a call to imitation based on a hierarchical view of authority. Jesus has washed their feet, and he is greater than they are. So if the greater does this, how much more the lesser. The ones sent and the servants should imitate the master and the one sending. However, there is a "tricky" spiritual logic at work. Jesus is claiming privilege, but it is not the privilege of exemption. He is saying that he is first and they must follow him. He is using his revered position to undercut what usually accompanies revered positions — dominance of others. His footwashing was not an act of condescension on his part, but the announcement of a new social order. This order is structured on mutual service rather than social preference. He is first and he is acting last. Therefore, the categories of first and last are shattered. In their place is reciprocal interdependence.

However, this text is more than a proposal for an ideal community. Its underlying dynamic is the intimate link between knowing and doing. If people try to do things without the proper accompanying understanding, the doing is not authentic. The inner world of knowing and the outer world of doing are not in sync. People are washing the feet of one another, but they note that one footwasher is better than another. The inner world of competitive power and status remains. We are still in the world of first and last and a scale of relative rating in between. What has changed is the content of the competitive ranking. Now the question is: who is the best servant? This is as wrong-headed an approach as the disciples' question: "Who is the greatest in the kingdom of heaven?" (Matt. 18:1). This inner discrepancy in relation to outer action always plagues "religious" activity.

Competitive status is a built-in mental mechanism. It is not easily modified, and, in my estimation, it is never erased. There is a story that underlines its pervasiveness. A priest knelt in the first pew of the church and prayed to God, "Lord, have mercy on me, a sinner." A deacon kneeling next to him repeated the prayer, "Lord, have mercy on me, a sinner." There was a noise in the back of the church. The priest and the deacon turned around. In the back pew was the janitor. He prayed, "Lord, have mercy on me, a sinner." The priest turned to the deacon and said, "Look who thinks he's a sinner!" The drive to be first is ever-present, even when it is first in the world of sin.

If Jesus is proposing a community beyond the compulsion to dominance and competition, he must show us the way. Imitating his action without knowing his inner orientation will result in washing feet as an act of subtle self-promotion. However, when the story is taken as a whole, it does suggest a path to authentic service. Authentic service is not something you immediately do. It is something you eventually get to. It demands an inner transformation that manifests itself in the outer world. Strangely enough, the path to service is gratitude. Said another way, originality is the antidote for competition.

How does this work?

Jesus' service of his disciples is a result of his inner God-consciousness. He is in touch with the Divine Source and is receiving divine energies. This inner awareness fills him with gratitude. His life is not his own. It is realized as a dynamic relationship of origin, destiny, and present moment. This realization fills him and he is about to spill over. "From his fullness we have all received" (John 1:16). Although the story does not mention it explicitly, I imagine Jesus had to focus on the nitty-gritty aspects of toes, arches, and heels in order to wash feet. However, this focus on feet did not replace his God-consciousness. Jesus had dual consciousness. He remembered who he was — a God-grounded, God-given, God-manifesting person — as he went about the task of essential service. This means he washed feet out of an inner fullness. He simply gave as he was receiving.

In spiritual teaching this inner awareness is the true source of action. Human need may be the context and condition, but it is not the primary driver. When we know ourselves in this graced way, we recognize this graced possibility in others and move toward them in a way that will awaken this inner reality. Service done from a spiritual center does have a hidden agenda. But it is not the agenda of competitive status. It is the agenda of awakening the soul through attending to the body, mind, or social condition. The complete care of an attending human person grounded in God is meant to awaken the self-giving of God in the depths of all people. In the last analysis, when all the intermediaries are acknowledged and honored, the startling truth is seen clearly, usually for only a moment before it returns to hiddenness. It is God who acts in us and God in other people who receives our actions.

If you know these things, then this blessedness that you are will overflow

> like a fountain inside you
> like a harvest white and ready
> like a light breaking through
> like a grape bursting from a vine
> like a woman giving birth

and you will do them.

A First Reflection: The Strength of Never

I keep coming back to Peter's resistance, his refusal to let Jesus wash his feet. There is something fundamental to the human condition in the hard words, "You will never wash my feet." There is an adamance in that "never" that resonates in most human hearts. To pun around, Peter is putting his foot down so he will not have to have his foot washed. Jesus has gone too far this time. Is this intimacy too much for Peter? His "no" is said with his back to the wall. What we have expressed in these words is the ultimate inner barrier to receiving divine love.

Right before her death Elizabeth of the Trinity wrote a letter to her superior. One phrase appeared again and again, "Let yourself be loved...LET yourself be loved...LET yourself be loved." The emphasis is not on love or self but on letting. We resist "letting" it happen. This indicates that we do not have to do anything as much as we have to stop doing something. Something will happen if we can just keep from pushing it away. But in order to let go we have to understand why we hold on. Something of great importance must be at stake.

In his book *Facing West from California's Shores* David Toolan tells a story about one group session of a month-long program entitled titled "Birth, Sex, and Death."* This session focused on an exercise developed by the British psychologist Ronald Laing. "The group simulates a tight birth canal, webbing themselves together in a line to form a pressurized tunnel wall. The candidate for birthing, stripped and oiled, then elbow-crawls, squirms through." At the finish the candidate had to rest and allow himself to be loved, not for what he had done but just for being. One All-American candidate vigorously squirmed through, but he was unable to handle the gratuitous love that attends all births. "Finally tears came, and he was asked to look into the faces of those around him, few of whom did not see their own sore hearts in his confusion, his resistance to being loved for no ulterior purpose...." I think this incident names a large part of the resistance — being loved for no ulterior purpose.

We attach ourselves to our deeds. We hang our résumés on our souls. We coax intimates to tell us *why* they love us. We want to tie their feeling to some quality we possess. Our loveability is a product we have produced. If someone loves us for our being and not our doing, this whole carefully constructed world of self-promotion crumbles. If divine love is unconditional, not considering our list of virtues and vices, what does this mean for our psychological and moral energies? What will we busy ourselves with? If divine love is not an isolated action but a state of being and we are included in that state, where does that lead?

To the secret we sometimes see, and then not.

A Second Reflection: Spirit Is Waiting

Spiritual exercises propose a certain sequence of outer and/or inner actions. If we follow them, certain inner spaces will open, certain realizations will occur, certain levels of being and consciousness will develop. The proof is in the pudding. The exercises may have been created by a major spiritual player and endorsed

---

*David Toolan, *Facing West from California's Shores* (New York: Crossroad, 1987).

by saints and prophets. Yet their value for any individual is whether their path is your path. Does this "practice" produce the desired results?

For me one of the most important aspects of spiritual exercises is their ability to show how certain spiritual states can be realized. All religious traditions contain strong imperative language — "Be loving" or "Be compassionate" or "Open yourself to receive God's love." However, the path to love, compassion, and the reception of divine love is often not marked out. It is frustrating to be bombarded with spiritual injunctions and not know how to "get there." It is the spiritual equivalent of the forbidding sign on the side of boxes: "Some Assembly Required." Inside there are no instructions. Spiritual injunctions demand spiritual directions.

Once a woman came to see me who had listened to a tape I had done with a psychologist. On the tape we had discussed the issue of self-esteem from psychological and spiritual perspectives. I mentioned many of the ideas explored in this book, in particular that the deeper self is grounded in Spirit and that grounding is the source of self-worth. First, she rehearsed these ideas to make sure that she had understood them. (She was much more concrete about them than I was.) Then, she said, "Fine, how do I do it?" She wanted to know how to take a spiritual idea and turn it into a personal realization. She was looking for a spiritual exercise.

The powerful revelation that God is a passionate love who desires to wash our feet only so that we can walk in the ways of Light needs a spiritual exercise to help us "get there," to realize this revelation. Many exercises have been devised. But there is one in the gospel of Luke that intrigues me. It is not often appreciated as a spiritual exercise, but I read it that way.

In general, Luke takes us through desire, prayer, and three persuasive pieces of rhetoric — a story, a set of injunctions, and a personal scrutiny — to open us up. He thinks if he can persuade us about what is waiting, we will reach for it. There is no doubt in his mind that the moment we reach is the moment we receive.

Desire. The eleventh chapter of Luke begins with Jesus at prayer. His disciples are watching him. When he finishes, they ask him to teach them to pray. They "spy" on Jesus at prayer because they realize prayer is the inner energy of his outer action. This is the activity that empowers him. In the outer world he takes long strides. He teaches the people, confronts religious leaders, heals the sick, and is clearheaded about his identity and mission. They want to be able to be this way, only they stumble when they try to teach, they are afraid of the religious leaders, they both pity and shrink from the sick, and they are unclear about their identity and mission. They see in prayer the possibility of their transformation.

Watching Jesus has created a desire in them. They want to receive life from God so they can give life to others. Desire is created by seeing. Therefore, it is important to look at the right people and cultivate the right set of desires. That is one of the reasons that spiritual teachers are "held up." The rest of us can see in them a human possibility that is very attractive. Spend some time looking at Jesus and desiring what he desires. Without desire the exercise may decline into dilettantism.

To their great credit, the disciples act on their desire. They ask, "Lord, teach us to pray."

Prayer. Jesus gives them a tightly worded and very short prayer. In fact, it is often prejudicially called the shortened version of the Lord's Prayer. The longer version and the one Christianity has formally adopted is in Matthew's gospel. Luke's terseness is:

Father,
Holy is your name.
Your kingdom come.
Give us each day our daily bread.
Forgive us our sins as we forgive everyone who is indebted
   to us.
Lead us not into temptation.

The brevity is the spiritual key. This is not a series of petitions to a reluctant God. This prayer does not "rattle on." These phrases are jabs, meant to cut through a false idea of prayer and open the speaker to a new possibility. They are not said by a creature frightened about surviving or a sinner worried about punishment. A beloved child of God speaks these words. They reflect a decentered ego and a recentered self, a self with the divine passion at its core. If the disciples wish to participate in the selfhood of Christ, the conversion that is necessary is reflected in this prayer. Panicky petitions are replaced by a sustained effort at openness to the divine life and intentionality.

This understanding of prayer is expressed in an interesting way by Henry and Regina Weiman:

> Certain attitudes of the personality are the outstretched wings of a bird which catch the wind in such a way that they are lifted into heights of the sky. Vultures soar into the blue until they are invisible, mounting in a spiral, but never moving their wings. Their outspread wings, while motionless, are kept adjusted to the upper currents of air in such a way that they are lifted ever higher. Certain attitudes of the personality are like those outstretched wings of the bird. Prayer is adjusting the personality to God in such a way that God can work more potently for good than he otherwise could, as the outstretched wings of a bird enable the rising currents to carry it to higher levels.

It is not often that prayer is compared to a vulture. The point of the comparison is how the bird adapts to air currents in order to rise higher. Prayer is a series of inner adjustments, attitudinal alterations, so that "God can work more potently for good than he otherwise could." Jesus will now suggest the inner work that is necessary.

Story. Next Luke has Jesus tell a story. The first line begins, "Can you imagine..." As in "Can you believe it?" or "This may sound a bit fantastic, but bear with me a while," or "Don't laugh! This could really happen." The storyteller himself is incredulous. This is the situation. A man goes to a friend of his at midnight (a friend of his, mind you!). Another friend of his has arrived at his house, and he has no food to share with him. He needs three loaves of bread. The friend he goes to refuses him the bread. His excuse is that the door is locked and he is in bed with his children. (Just where is this man's wife?) Now the storyteller takes an uppity tone and closes with a "Let me give you the real scoop about this" remark. If he doesn't get up and give him the bread out of friendship, he will give him the bread to avoid being shamed.

Scholars stress that the setting of this story is village life. Hospitality for traveling friends is assumed. To refuse it is unthinkable. But this story begins by thinking the unthinkable and then taking it back. The friend (sic!) will give eventually — if not out of friendship than out of a fear of being shamed. Once the entire village knew about his refusal, he would be ostracized. Now if that is the way it is with the reluctant giver who still gives, what would it be with a reality whose essence is to give? Bottom line: if you ask for bread to feed others, you are going to get it.

This story is designed to assure the listener that divine reality is poised and ready to give. The response will never be, "Do not bother me. The door is locked." God is not asleep with his children. God is awake with his children, attending to their hungers. This is the first major adjustment. Realize what you are in the presence of.

Injunctions. "So ask and you will receive; seek and you will find; knock and the door will be opened to you. For everyone who asks, receives; and the one who seeks, finds; and to the one who knocks, the door will be opened." It must be stressed that the asking, seeking, and knocking do not make God attentive. They make us open and receptive. The story shapes consciousness in such a way that it is convinced it will not be rejected. The assumed problem is timidity. We are fearful to ask because we will be disappointed. If we can be assured of the generosity of God, we will ask, seek, and knock. Bread will fall into our hands. There are no locked doors, and there is no sleeping God.

Personal scrutiny. Now this interior mental exercise takes a different yet complementary turn. We are out of the story world and into our own personal world. Jesus is about to tell us a truth of our own personal experience. "What father among you would hand his son a snake when he asks for a fish? What mother among you would hand her daughter a scorpion when she asks for an egg?" (I modified the text to give both genders equal time.) The answer is, "No parent would do that." We would not deceive our children. It is said by those with strong imaginations that a fish looks something like a snake and an egg looks something like a scorpion. So substituting one for the other would be an act of deception. We would not give our children something harmful when they asked for something beneficial. However, the "kicker" is yet to come.

"If you then, who are wicked, know how to give good gifts to your children, now much more will the Father in heaven give the Holy Spirit to those who ask him." For the purposes of this exercise we are to acknowledge our chronic failures at enacting the good. We are not good people. We scheme and fight and cheat and, if we have to, do worse. But when it comes to our own, we know what to do. Our children receive good gifts. Where does this sudden burst of love in the midst of wickedness come from? Could it be that it is a dim reflection of a heavenly parent giving to us?

In the first story a man gave out of the fear of being shamed, and in this personal examination we discover we give good things to our children even though we are not good. Giving is built into us. It is built into us and emerges even if we resist it or are highly selective about it. This dynamism of giving exists in us in our imperfect state. In God it exists in a perfect state. There are no blocks and there is no selectivity in God. God gives. So ask, seek, and knock.

What will happen?

The Holy Spirit will arrive. That is who is waiting. Let's face it — there is some disappointment in this prospect. We usually ask God for little red wagons and twenty thousand until the end of the year. We plead for pain to be relieved and opportunity to present itself. We have a long list, a short list, and a prioritized list. Spirit seldom makes the cut. It is the last thing we think we need. Asking for the Holy Spirit is the final and most difficult adjustment of this exercise.

The thing about a spiritual exercise is that you have to do it. You cannot just think about it and say it won't work. So start with desire. Nurture it. Really want the life you see streaming through Jesus Christ. Say the prayer. Want to be in touch with God and the world. Say the prayer again. Mean it. Now notice that giving is everywhere. It is not quite the stingy world you have constructed in your head. Sure — some people are shamed into it, and some can only give to their immediate families. We are not talking perfection. But giving keeps breaking out. It keeps breaking out because the source of life is always giving.

So do not play it so safe. Ask with all your heart. Seek with all your heart. Knock with all your heart.

You will have to make up your own words. Let them reflect the insights you have garnered as you worked through the spiritual exercise.

Spirit will arrive, bringing to you a life you can only give away. The gospel is confident this will happen. The reason for this confidence is that Spirit is always present. It is we who are absent. This exercise just tries to tell us who is there so we will have the courage to open up.

Chapter 8

The Road Less Traveled
Is the Road Back

LUKE 22:14, 19–20; 24:13–35; 22:39–53

MYSTERY STORIES often begin with a single incident — Aunt Mildred's cat is found strangled, a sports car is abandoned on a deserted beach, a man reads an account of the closing of a diamond mine in South Africa and leaves the room immediately, etc. We do not know the meaning of the incident. We do know that as the story develops more information will be given and other events will happen. Eventually, the incident will be connected to other incidents and placed in a context in which it makes sense. The mystery will be solved.

Theorists contend that mystery and meaning are closely linked. Meaning comes about by connecting a part with a whole, and new meaning comes about by connecting this same part with larger and larger wholes. Contexts escalate. Therefore, a solved mystery on one level can become part of an unsolved mystery on another level. A physical mystery of *how* a person died can be solved, only to become part of a larger social mystery of *who* did it. "Who did it" can be solved, only to become part of the larger psychological mystery of "*Why* did he do it?" This can be solved, only to become part of a larger spiritual/theological mystery of how the divine-human enterprise is involved in this happening. In general, as contexts escalate mystery deepens. The physical is solved more easily than the social, the social more easily than the psychological, and the psychological more easily than the spiritual. When it comes to the ultimate context of the spiritual, the rumor is that when the meaning is seen, the event becomes more mysterious. The spiritual dimension of life is essentially mysterious. The more we know about it, the more mysterious it becomes.

Since this mystery-meaning process occurs in time, it implies that we are always looking back at events and interpreting them in the light of what we now know and are experiencing. When something is happening, we give it enough meaning to guide our response to it. However, afterward we may look back and see it in a new light. Our original meaning may have been accurate, but it was also partial. Now we see it in a larger context, and so change our minds and our behavior. Although the past is, to put it delicately, "done and gone," the present can redetermine its meaning. We can see a deeper level and be consoled. Or we can see a deeper level and be confounded. Kierkegaard was correct when he ventured, "We live forward, but we understand backward." Or in the jazzy image of Marshall McLuhan, "We drive into the future looking through the rear-view mirror."

This "piece of theory" about mystery and meanings over time is a fine filter to view the crucial event of Christian revelation. The crucifixion of Jesus has been investigated from many different points of view. It has been prosecuted from a physical perspective. Although historical and physical evidence is hard to come by, interested people have speculated that the medical cause of Jesus' death was most probably asphyxiation. To some Christians this may seem a wrong-headed approach or even, given the delicacy of some docetist positions, a blasphemy. But in a time when medical models are highly developed and highly valued, it is inevitable that they would be applied to Jesus.

The mystery of Jesus' death considerably deepens when the concerns are social and psychological. Was Pilate or Herod or the chief priests or the Sadducee party as a whole responsible for Jesus' death? And why was he executed? Because he claimed to be the Son of God? Because he reinterpreted the covenant demands to understand Israel as a mission to the Gentiles? Because he attacked the theory and actual practice of the temple? Because he was mistakenly or rightly thought to be a political revolutionary? The gospel stories of Jesus' dying are primarily concerned with spiritual/theological meaning. But this meaning is not the first to present itself. The glaring meaning of "social failure" has to be worked through before the deeper meaning of divine revelation can be appreciated.

Solving the mystery of the spiritual meaning of Jesus' suffering and dying is what the story of the road to Emmaus is all about. The two people making their way toward Emmaus are in the process of working through one interpretation of the sufferings and death of Jesus and beginning to appreciate something very strange and very powerful. But before we can walk with them and receive this great spiritual teaching, we have to return to an earlier episode in the gospel of Luke. Jesus prepared his apostles for his death by providing them with the clue to its deeper spiritual meaning. However, the clue was not fully understood the first time it was given. We will "lift out" a few crucial passages from what has come to be known as the Last Supper.

> *When the hour had come, Jesus took his place at table with his apostles. And he said to them, "With desire have I desired to eat this Passover with you before I suffer."*...

The "hour" is the time when the revelation of Jesus will be seen in its most intense and dramatic form. His ministry has been an ongoing revelation of the kingdom of God. However, the summary and symbol of it all is called "the hour." The hour is the crucifixion of Christ. The spiritual teaching of Jesus will paradoxically be revealed and concealed in this event. The key to this revelation and concealment is in the meal. That is why it is Jesus' overwhelming desire to eat this meal with them *before* he suffers. This is the one of the oldest and most venerable connections of Christian faith. If you do not "get" the meal, you will not "get" the cross. If you do not "get" the cross, you will not "get" the meal. Eucharist and cross are two sides of the same coin.

This opening desire of Jesus unfolds into the central action. This action is the key to the deepest identity of Jesus. However, it is an action that is not easy to read but, as it turns out, is easy to forget.

> *... He took bread and giving thanks he broke it and gave it to them, saying, "This is my body that is given for you. Do this in memory of me."*

This is the symbolic gesture and words that reveal the truth about Jesus and the truth about his sufferings. It is not straight-forward. It needs to be pondered and to be comprehended. In this way when its meaning breaks through, it will have the qual-ity of revelation. Something that was not seen will be seen, the concealed will be revealed, scales will fall from the eyes. "Aha" will happen, then not happen. Spiritual sight is difficult to maintain.

The bread is Jesus' body, his enfleshed life. He takes it into his hands. This is the peculiar capacity we all have. We can move deeper than partial choices and actions. We can gather ourselves up as a whole, ready ourselves for a gesture that is an expres-sion of the whole person, an action that carries the complete self into the visible world. Once his whole life is in his hands, he gives thanks. This is the key. Gratitude defines his deepest sense of himself. His life is not his own. He is receiving life at every second from the Divine Source. He does not possess or control who he is. Jesus' deepest self is not a freestanding entity but a relationship with his heavenly Father, the transcendent source of generating love.

When we initially sense we are not our own, our anxiety in-creases. Our usual sense of self-possession is dispelled. In its place is only a radical openness to a life-giving source. We have no con-trol over this source, no contract for its services, and no right we can stand on and make demands. We are at its mercy. We have no recourse but to trust that its flow of life and love will continue. Then as our inner appreciation of this radical trust at the core of the human condition deepens, a switch, sometimes sudden and sometimes gradual, occurs. We move from anxiety and hesitant trust into gratitude. This is what some thinkers call ontological gratitude. We are grateful for being itself, for the life and love that pulses through us right now. Regrets about past mistakes do not preoccupy us. Worries about the future do not paralyze us.

We are now, here, alive. And suddenly we are thankful, grateful, and, most importantly of all, filled.

The spiritual benefit of gratitude is that it fills us up from the inside. The tears that often accompany deeply felt gratitude are spillage. They are the overflow of interior fullness. This is the first moment of eucharistic identity. We gather our life as given to us from beyond ourselves and are completely filled by gratitude. It is out of this fullness that we then break the bread. We cannot give ourselves out of emptiness or out of ego or out of carefully calculated motives. Eucharistic breaking comes from grateful fullness. It is the simple, natural, free move of full people.

The process of giving entails the act of breaking. One of the best images for this spiritual necessity is the prism. The single ray of light strikes the prism and it splinters into a full spectrum of colors. Our deep interior contact with the Divine Source has the quality of singleness or oneness about it. "Blessed are the single-hearted for they shall see God" (Matt. 5:8). This is the soul as it opens into and unites with the boundless world of spirit. But as the soul mediates that boundless spirit into the mind, the body, and out into the world, it becomes bounded, finite, detailed, particular. In other words, it breaks into pieces under the pressure of finite particularity. Our infinite lives are always given in finite ways. When the deepest center of the human person receives the Infinite Spirit and yearns to pass it on into the world, breaking is the path it travels as it gives itself.

In the act of giving the bread the deeper identification is made. "This is my body given for you." When bread is eaten, it enters the person and builds the person up from the inside. Of course, as Jesus remarks so realistically in a quite different context, some of it goes into the ditch. However, the symbolic point is that Jesus' giving goes into the interior of the person and builds up the person from within. In a different image, the new covenant is written on the hearts of people. The former covenant that was written on stone was always "outside" commandments that had to be obeyed in fear of punishment and in hope of reward. This new covenant will be a communion with God in the soul that will burst forth in action. Jesus is coming from the deepest center of himself, a center where he is sustained by the divine spirit, and he desires to reach that same center in others and revivify it with what he has to give. Jesus is life poured into life so that other life can grow strong. This is the intent of the breaking and the giving.

People are to do this with one another. When they do, Jesus will be remembered. "Do this in memory of me." These are the simple yet important instructions. Although they are often seen as an afterthought to the more dramatic eucharistic action, they are crucial to the dynamics of Luke's story. First, people will remember Jesus in a variety of ways. Some of these ways will be inadequate to his full reality and will have to be corrected by this particular eucharistic memory. Secondly, it is this memory that will provide the clue to the sufferings. Without it the sufferings may appear meaningless. Thirdly, this memory is really the performance of an action. In the performance of the action the memory becomes presence. It is no longer a retrieval of the past, but a present experience of the living Christ. Without this way of memory and presence the resurrection of Christ becomes a ghostly event. "Do this in memory of me" is a constitutive part of the eucharistic identity of Christ and of those who would follow his way and receive his wisdom.

However, they do not remember Jesus in this way. The supper revelation and its urgent imperative fades. What takes its place is the sleeping in Gethsemane and then arrest, trial, crucifixion, death, and the testimony of the women that the tomb is empty. In the fleeing and the fear what are they to make of it all? As he had predicted, they struck the shepherd and the sheep scattered. Now would be the time to remember him as he had told them. But they forget the instructions. Instead they fall prey to more conventional forms of remembering, remembering that leaves them sad and confused. Before long they are walking away from the revelation of the cross, unsure about who Jesus was, about what was happening in his sufferings and death, and about who they were as his followers. They need another lesson in the art of memory and presence, a lesson that will uncover the meaning and mystery of the cross. It is about to be given to them.

That same day two of them were making their way toward Emmaus, a village seven miles from Jerusalem.

In Luke's gospel all the resurrection stories happen "on the same day." The women and Peter going to the tomb, the two on the way to Emmaus, the appearance to the disciples in Jerusalem, and the ending of the gospel with the disciples praying in the temple are a single flow of events. This means they are all part of the same spiritual experience. Each episode is integral to the whole revelation.

These two travelers are not out for an idle stroll. The fact that there are two of them probably indicates they are Christian missionaries. Christian missionaries were sent out two by two. However, they are moving toward Emmaus. This is a strange destination for any follower of Jesus. Scholars are unsure about the exact location of Emmaus. Some think that it might have been the site of a Roman garrison, built around a pool of water. If this is the case, the symbolic goal of their journey is that they are moving toward Roman power. Roman power was displayed in the death of Jesus, and to the victor goes the spoils. The spoils in this situation are the followers of Jesus.

The symbolic significance of this movement toward Emmaus is underlined by the geographic information that it is a movement away from Jerusalem. In Luke's gospel avoiding Jerusalem is avoiding the true path of Christ. The whole gospel is a journey toward Jerusalem, the revelation takes place in Jerusalem, and the story ends in Jerusalem. Walking away from Jerusalem and toward Emmaus means that they are abandoning the "unworldly" power of Christ displayed in his passion and death and embracing the "worldly" power of Rome that killed him. They are not travelers but deserters, not people on a mission but people walking away from a cause.

We call this story "The Road to Emmaus," but they never arrive at Emmaus. Just as well. If they walked through the gates of Emmaus, they would be within the walls of Rome and the way of life that Roman rule symbolizes. Then the real failure would not be the death of Jesus but their own inability to comprehend the spiritual truth hidden in his social and political suffering and dying. The more appropriate title for this story is "The Road Back to Jerusalem." But the road back is also the road less traveled. Before they turn and return, something must happen.

> *They were talking to each other about all the things that had happened.*

They are remembering Jesus. He told them how to remember him. "Take bread, give thanks, break it, give it to one another, saying, 'This is my body given for you.'" Are they remembering him in this way or are they using some other mode of recollection?

> *And it happened while they were talking and discussing with one another Jesus drew near and went with them. But their eyes were kept from recognizing him.*

"It happened" — the unplanned accompaniment by Jesus who goes unrecognized. This unrecognized Jesus is the storyteller's mystical device that will be the catalyst for the conversion of the two disillusioned followers. There is always the temptation to interpret this "unrecognizability" as a physical limitation. Their eyes were cloudy and they could not quite make out who this sudden fellow traveler was. Perhaps even God caused this ocular blindness for a deeper purpose.

However, their inability to recognize Jesus is not a physical defect. There is no physical description of Jesus in the gospels. Although the early church thought Jesus was the most important person ever to live, they did not physically describe him in their writings. There is a spiritual reason for this failure to tell us his height, weight, bearing, and, of course, the color of his eyes. Physical descriptions apply to individuals but not to persons. Persons are not known by description but by action. The reason the two do not recognize Jesus is not because their eyes cannot pick up his physical characteristics. They do not recognize him because they have forgotten his characteristic gesture. The person of Jesus is summed up and symbolized by an action, an action he did with them and told them to do with one another, an action that is the key to the mystery of his suffering. They have forgotten this action. Therefore, they do not recognize him.

> *And he said to them, "What are you talking about with each other as you walk along?"*
> *They stood still looking sad.*
> *One of them, Cleopas by name, answered him, "Are you the only stranger in Jerusalem that does not know the things that have happened there in these days?"*
> *And he said to them, "What things?"*

The fellow traveler inquires about their conversation. So far in the story we have been told they are discussing what has happened, but we do not know the tone of the discussion. Jesus' question causes them to stop walking, and we are told that they are sad. Whatever they are talking about, it is not causing them any happiness.

We are given the name of one, but not the other. Is the reader/listener of this story asked to become the second traveler? Are we asked to journey from a conventional understanding of the death of Jesus that causes sadness to a deeper understanding of his death that causes joy? Is this a story about everyone's temptation in the face of what seems like senseless suffering and dying to escape to a more secure and more powerful space?

Cleopas's question is deeply ironic. Jesus is the only one who does know what has happened in Jerusalem. His two dialogue partners have no idea of the deeper meaning of what has happened in Jerusalem. In a moment they will demonstrate their ignorance in a lengthy recitation of the facts culminating in a statement of complete community blindness. Cleopas calls the unrecognized Jesus a "stranger in Jerusalem." This harkens back to his birth when "in the city of David there was no room at the inn." In one way Jesus is a true son of Jerusalem. He is the fulfillment of the law and the prophets. He is most at home in the temple where as a child of twelve he taught "his Father's business." Yet in another way he is a stranger. The ruling elite do not recognize him, and they crucify him outside the walls. The conundrum of the story is embodied in the phrase "stranger in Jerusalem."

Jesus simply responds, "What things?" He invites them to tell him what had happened to him in Jerusalem. They are now going to remember him. It is a rule of thumb to be leery when a spiritual teacher asks you a question. They are going to see more in what you say than you had intended. These two sad people unload their grief at length.

> *They said to him, "The things about Jesus of Nazareth, a prophet powerful in word and deed before God and all the people...*

This is a true but partial appraisal of Jesus. He is a prophet, but more profoundly he is the Son of God. What happened to him is not just one more murder of a prophet. It is also true that he was held in high esteem by God and by many people. However, this description also runs the risk of reducing him to a reputation. Their memory is already askew.

> *...and how our chief priests and rulers delivered him up to be condemned to death, and crucified him.*

They remembered him as a victim. The chief priests did something *to* him. He was not an active player in his own death. He was the passive recipient of the condemnation of others. Their lack of understanding is beginning to show.

> *We had hoped that he was the one to redeem Israel.*

They remembered him as an ethnocentric messiah. But Jesus was not sent only to Israel. He was, as it were, sent through Israel to all people. We now know why they are sad. Their hopes have been dashed. However, what they hoped for was never what Jesus was sent for. His mission and their expectations are not in sync.

> *Besides all this, it is now the third day since these things have happened.*

They mention the "third day." The reader/listener gets the impression that for them it is a simple matter of counting. The number "3" is a factual statement. But the reader/listener knows the number "3" is symbolic. This is the day of the revelation. This is the day they will understand.

Also some women of our company amazed us.

Amazement is a first step in the process of spiritual perception. But it is only a first step. Eventually they must "see." Their predicament is that they cannot recognize Jesus. Amazement by itself does not bring sight, and sight is what is needed.

> *They were at the tomb early in the morning. They did not find his body. They came back saying they had seen a vision of angels who said he was alive. Some of those who were with us went to the tomb, and found it just as the women had said, but him they did not see."*

They have all the facts and none of the meaning. This series of observations culminates their memory of Jesus and caps off their litany of misunderstandings. They have remembered him as a reputation, a victim, and a failure. Now they remember him as a dead man. They go to the land of the dead to find the living. They gather at the place where he is not, thinking his body (his reality) must be there.

The storyteller has given these two sad followers a lot of "air time." They are given many lines, each one further contributing to the gathering darkness of their minds. The last phrase, "him they did not see," is not another entry. It is the conclusion of their confusion. When you remember Jesus as a reputation, a victim, a failure, and a dead man, "him you will not see."

> *And he said to them, "O how foolish you are and slow of heart to believe all that the prophets have spoke. Was it not necessary that the Christ suffer all these things and enter into his glory?"*

Jesus is not happy. It is hard to read these two sentences and not conclude that they are the words of a ticked-off resurrected Christ. He does not appreciate how they have remembered him. He calls them foolish. The fool says in his heart there is no God.

In other words, the foolish person tries to interpret and establish life without considering the spiritual dimension. These two have interpreted Jesus in strictly sociopolitical terms. They have neglected the spiritual perspective he tried to communicate to them at the supper. Therefore, they are foolish.

Also, they are slow of heart. In biblical spirituality the heart is connected to the eyes. When the heart burns, the fire pushes up the chest and flows out the eyes. This allows the person to see. The eyes are like the headlights of a car. They are lit from within in order to peer into the darkness without. When the fire in the heart dies down, the person's sight dims and eventually goes out. This may be poor physiology, but it is good spirituality. When people are not in touch with their deepest center (the heart), they cannot see the events of life from a spiritual perspective. On the physical level they may have 20–20 vision. But on the spiritual level they are visually impaired. The path to spiritual sight is to stir the embers of the heart. This is precisely the strategy of Jesus.

Their foolishness and sluggish hearts are the result of their failure to penetrate into the deepest meaning of prophesy. The story does not elaborate on what the prophets spoke. It only suggests that the glory of Christ inevitably entails suffering. "Was it not necessary" is a powerful phrase. It recalls what the prodigal father told the older son. "It was necessary to rejoice and be glad, for this your brother was dead, and is alive. He was lost, and now is found" (Luke 15:31). We are at the center of the mystery. Jesus seems to be saying, "Don't you see? It had to be this way." At this moment in the story it is clear they do not see. They are uncomprehending and sad. Only with more meditation will we be able to say, "We see!"

> *And beginning with Moses and all the prophets, he interpreted to them in all the scriptures the things concerning himself.*

These two are treated to a tour of scripture by Christ himself. It is part of the storytelling perversity of Luke that he tells us *that* Jesus told them, but he does not tell us *what* Jesus told them. I, for one, am interested and have often thought this story could be profitably expanded at this point. But the principle is: the story-teller has given us everything we need to appropriate the spiritual perspective that is being developed. So although the content of what Jesus told them is crucial, the storyteller has other "fish to fry." The focus is not on what he is saying, but on what is happening to them as he is talking to them and interpreting the scripture. We will not find out what is happening to them until a little later in the story.

> *So they drew near to the village to which they were going. He appeared to be going further. But they urged him, saying, "Remain with us, for evening is near and the day is nearly over."*
> *So he went in to remain with them.*

The two are getting close to the destination of their original intent. They are not there, but they are drawing near. Jesus is not going there. He is journeying further. Why does he "appear to be going further"? It may be he is still unhappy with their faulty memory of him. They have said nothing to show they have come to a better perspective. It may be that Jesus is on his way to the ends of the earth. His risen mission is universal. He will tell whoever he meets. Those who understand will follow along and those who do not will stop. Whatever the reason for the seeming separation, it is forestalled by one urgent, simple plea, "Remain with us."

This is a crucial move in becoming a disciple of Jesus. Jesus always walks further. He outdistances his followers. However, once you ask him to stay, he immediately replies. This is because the invitation to remain shows an openness to him. What he has already told you is fascinating enough to want more. Both Jesus and his Father never refuse an invitation. The reason the two have asked him to remain is that "evening is near and the day is nearly over." In other words, it is time to eat and this has always been a special moment for Jesus. He characterized himself as bread. So when people are hungry, he is eager to be with them. There is very little doubt about what he will do at supper.

When he was at table with them, he took the bread, blessed it, broke it, and gave it to them. And their eyes were opened and they recognized him. He became invisible from among them.

Jesus now repeats what he did at the supper before he suffered. He engages in his characteristic gesture, the action that reveals the truth about him and his sufferings. This action — repeated after his suffering and after their misinterpretation of his suffering and after Jesus' reinterpretation of his suffering in the light of Moses and the prophets — is understood. Their eyes are opened and they understand. The next line is often translated, "he vanished out of their sight." The same Greek word — *egeneto* — is used as when he drew near to them. So his entrance into and exit from the story can be viewed as a special moment of manifestation. At the beginning this manifestation is unrecognized, and then when it is recognized, it disappears. The risen Christ has "done his job." He has brought his community to a deeper realization and taught them, a second time, to remember him correctly. Exit Jesus.

Is there a spiritual meaning to Christ's disappearance? If the story is a literary form geared to promote a spiritual sensitivity, the suspicion is that there is a reason for his sudden vanishing. Christ becomes invisible as a character in the story when the truth of his identity is seen. Christ always was and now is the ultimate source of wisdom and communion among his followers. He is present whenever and wherever he is remembered correctly. The correct remembrance has to do with performing the characteristic gesture within the community. Whenever the divine life wells up in one person and is poured into another person so that that person is built up from within by that gift of life, then Jesus is present as the invisible power and energy of that relationship. He is no longer one more visible, physical entity among them. Nor is he in the tomb. Nor is he a ghost. He is the invisible spirit of their communion. The key to finding the risen Christ is knowing where to look.

But as important as this moment of recognition is, it leaves us still searching. What did they see and how did what they see reverse their reading of his sufferings and death?

But the story is relentlessly pursuing another direction, a direction that is concerned not with the content of what they saw but with the process they went through in order to see it.

> *They said to each other, "Did not our hearts burn within us as he talked to us on the way, and opened to us the scriptures?"*

This is the reason they could see him. Their hearts, their spiritual centers, were awakened. Previously, they were sluggish and therefore spiritually myopic. Now with their spiritual center awake they can see the world of spirit. The way this happened is that the scriptures were opened up. The purpose of the scripture is to burn the heart. Once the heart burns, the eyes are opened to see the spiritual dimension of what is taking place. It is only on the level of spirit that the suffering, death, and resurrection of Jesus can be understood. This understanding takes place on the way. The way is the attempt to follow after Jesus, to apprentice ourselves to his life, to walk behind him and try not to be afraid.

> *That same hour they rose up and returned to Jerusalem.*

This is the "hour" that was mentioned at the beginning of the Last Supper episode: "When the hour came..." It is the "same hour" because the same revelation has taken place. Only this time the indication is that they understood it. They "rose up" means that they share in the resurrection of Jesus. Resurrection may be understood, in the first moment, as an event in the life of Jesus. But it is equally an event in the life of the early followers of Jesus. Their resurrection is that they participate in the fullness of spirit that Jesus revealed and communicated. This participation turns them back to the sufferings and crucifixion that they had been walking away from. They never enter Emmaus and the worldly power of Rome because they finally understand the unworldly power of Jesus' suffering in Jerusalem.

> *They found the eleven who were gathered together and those who were with them. They said, "The Lord has risen indeed, and has appeared to Simon."*
>
> *Then they told about what had happened on the road, and how he was known to them in the breaking of the bread.*

What happened to the two on the road is confirmed by the community in Jerusalem. It is not an isolated experience or an offbeat interpretation. The Lord is risen. This designation of Jesus as Lord may carry the weight of his new form of presence. This presence manifests itself to people. Although we do not have the account of the Lord appearing to Peter, we have the proclamation. This spurs the two to tell their story. They started their journey by discussing the things that had happened in Jerusalem. This discussion is now superseded by what happened on the road and their sudden discovery of the essence of Christ that transcends death. His resurrected presence is known in the action of breaking the bread.

✳

However, the mystery still lingers. The spiritual meaning of Jesus' death has not been brought to light. The symbolic action of the meal has been brought forward a second time and its revelation appreciated. Yet, this revelation has not been connected explicitly to the sufferings and death of Christ. The "Did you not know it was necessary . . . " still elicits a "I did not know it was necessary." Eucharist and cross have been brought together, but they have not dialogued with one another. In order for that to happen, we have to explore another story. We have to meditate on an episode that many scholars feel is the key to the death of Christ: the garden of Gethsemane.

> *And he came out and went, as was his custom, to the Mount of Olives. The disciples followed him.*

It is after the supper. Jesus is doing what he is in the habit of doing — going to the Mount of Olives to pray. St. Luke stresses Jesus' prayer activity throughout the gospel. It is the way he stays in touch with his Father, the way the will of God stays active in him. That the disciples are following him suggests they are going to learn something about prayer. More precisely, they are going to be offered a teaching. Learning may have to await another time. Perhaps on a road to Emmaus.

> *When he came to the place, he said to them, "Pray that you may not enter into temptation."*

This is the lesson. Prayer is a power *not* to do something. At this stage we do not know what the temptation is. But prayer will withhold our entering into it. Jesus is linking together prayer and resistance.

> *He withdrew from them about a stone's throw, and knelt down and prayed, "Father, if you are willing, remove this cup from me. Nevertheless, not my will but yours be done."*

On one level the image of a stone's throw suggests a short distance. On another level it is a harbinger of violence. And when it is connected to the image of cup, an atmosphere of violent suffering pervades the prayer of Christ. His prayer is complex, a delicate positioning of himself in relation to the ultimate source of Love he calls Father. If it is God's will, Jesus does not want to suffer. He does not court suffering nor is he neutral toward it. He does not want it. This line is meant to stop the sick searching after suffering of many Christians. However, whatever happens, Jesus wants to remain faithful to God's will.

Is God's will that Jesus suffer? No.

God's will is that Jesus manifest divine love and offer the possibility of reconciliation no matter what else is happening. If he is drinking a cup of suffering, he offers love and reconciliation. If he is drinking a cup of wedding wine, he offers love and reconciliation. The temptation to be resisted is to enter the world of violent suffering on the terms of those who are inflicting the suffering and not on the terms of his Father. Prayer is not losing the truth about yourself when everyone else has lost the truth about themselves.

> *And there appeared to him an angel from heaven, strengthening him. Being in agony he prayed more earnestly*

and his sweat became drops of blood falling down upon the earth. When he rose from prayer...

Before the athletic games trainers would work the muscles of the athletes. The athletes would break into a sweat and be warmed up, ready for the contest. This image of Jesus, the angel, and the sweat alludes to this athletic procedure. Jesus is about to enter into a contest. His prayer is his preparation. This is going to be a contest with the power of violence. So agony and blood are introduced into the picture. This prayer readies him, fills him with power. He began by kneeling. Now he rises, out of the earth, strong with the strength that comes from prayer, a strength unlike the force that will be brought against him.

> *...he came to his disciples and found them sleeping from sorrow. He said to them, "Why do you sleep? Rise and pray that you may not enter into temptation."*

Being awake and being asleep are discrete physical states. They are also used as images for discrete spiritual states. Being awake means staying in touch with your deepest spiritual center. This is what prayer does for Jesus. It keeps him in touch with his Father. Therefore, he is able to call upon this relationship in the situations that will develop. Being asleep is being out of touch with this spiritual center. Therefore, the disciples will mimic anything that is happening in the situation. They will have no power of resistance.

Furthermore, they are "sleeping from sorrow." This is a difficult phrase to grasp. It may mean that life is too much for them, and they have given up. They have lost their zest to compete in the games. Or it may mean that being out of touch with their spiritual center will bring them to sorrow. If this is the case, this phrase is not an unfair description of the two on the road to Emmaus. They have lost their spiritual perspective, and they are sad over what has happened. They have not stayed awake. Therefore, they have interpreted the death of Jesus as a tragic failure. Yet something more was going on, but their sleepy eyes and sluggish heart could not see it.

Jesus' prayer will keep him from entering temptation, and the disciples' sleeping will facilitate their entry into temptation. When the temptation arrives, it will be met by resistance and compliance. And the temptation is about to arrive.

While he was still speaking...

This means that what is about to happen is directly connected to the teaching on prayer that Jesus was attempting to show his disciples.

> *...behold a crowd and the one called Judas, one of the twelve, was leading them. He drew near to Jesus to kiss him. But Jesus said to him, "Judas, would you betray the Son of Man with a kiss?"*

The storyteller wants us to behold a crowd. The crowd will represent mob psychology. People will act in a mindless way, out of touch with their deepest selves and falling prey to violent tendencies. This crowd is led by Judas, one of Jesus' closest disciples. He has found an exquisitely appropriate way to betray Jesus. Jesus has stayed awake in prayer so that his interior relationship with his Father will govern his action in the outer world. The inside and outside of Jesus will be in harmony. This harmony is essential to anyone who would bring spirit into the world of action.

Judas ruptures this inner and outer connection. He is going to place an action in the outer world that is completely contradicted in his inner world. He attempts to kiss Jesus' hand as a sign of loyalty while interiorly he is bent on betrayal. Jesus' own unity makes him sensitive to this split in Judas. His comment to Judas is a form of love that Jesus often displays in the gospels. He shows Judas to himself for the possibility of conversion. "Do you see the hypocrisy you have fallen into, Judas? It is not too late to change."

> *When those who were with him saw what was going to happen, they said, "Lord, should we strike with the sword?" One of them struck the slave of the high priest and cut off his ear.*

> *But Jesus said, "No more of this!"*
> *He touched his ear and healed him.*

The disciples enter into temptation. They launch a preemptive strike. They see what is going to happen — the violent arrest of Jesus. They ask Jesus if they should respond in kind. But before he can answer, they have already struck. Violence is fast and mindless. If you are not prepared *not* to enter into it, you will quickly be engulfed by it. They have perceived and projected a violent outer world and entered into it on its own terms. This is entering into temptation. The result of falling asleep and not praying.

Jesus states simply yet firmly the will of the Father he has prayed into his very being. "No more of this!" They have cut off the ear of the slave of the high priest. This is a symbolic wound. The beginning of violence is the end of dialogue. When violence starts, people no longer talk and listen to one another. The disciples do not wait for Jesus to respond and they make it impossible for the slave of the high priest to hear them. But Jesus' entire ministry has been an attempt to give people ears. He has wanted them to hear and understand. He is not about to reverse that passion now. He does what he has done from the beginning. He heals ears so people can hear. He refuses the temptation to violence and remains faithful to the project of reconciliation. He is rising from prayer.

> *Then Jesus said to the chief priests and captains of the temple and elders who had come out against him, "Have you come out as against a robber, with swords and clubs? When I was with you day after day in the temple, you did not lay hands on me. But this is your hour, and the power of darkness."*

Jesus addresses the religious leaders and unmasks the power of darkness that inhabits them. They have made Jesus into something he is not in order to do to him what they wish. They have made him into a robber so they can use their swords and clubs. But his true identity, the identity he has in the temple, is the Son of God. When that identity is in place, they do not lay hands on him. No one ever harms the son or daughter of God. First the sons and daughters of God are turned into robbers. Then they are attacked and arrested. This is the power of darkness, for it clouds the truth with a lie, and then acts out the lie as if it were the truth. Jesus will not succumb to this strategy. He will remain a light in the darkness, a light the darkness cannot overcome.

Are we any closer to solving the mystery of meaning surrounding the crucifixion of Christ? Have the spiritual dynamics that the cross revealed come more clearly into view? At one point Paul says very succinctly, "God, in Christ, was reconciling the world to himself" (2 Cor. 5:19). Yes, it is about reconciliation. But what does that entail? Saying it is one thing. Exploring it is another thing. What do the narratives tell us about the complex spiritual dynamics of bringing together God and the world?

Jesus' deepest identity is his relationship to the Father which overflows into a mission of love to an alienated world. Whatever else Jesus is, he is this first and foremost. This makes him the Christ. What he desires is to give the life he is receiving from the Divine Source to other people. He is faithful to that task and his prayer keeps him in touch with this deepest identity and mission.

If there are any romantic inclinations in this identity and mission, they are quickly dispelled by the actual flow of events. Early in the gospel of Luke the test case of divine love and human alienation is envisioned. "If you love those who love you, what grace is there in that? For even sinners love those who love them" (Luke 6:32). Even people who are unconnected with the Divine Source repay in kind. Therefore, mutual love *may* be engendered by the power of divine self-giving, but it will not be the way divine love is shown forth to the world. Mutual love could just be another instance of the unexceptional banding together of like interests. "But love your enemies...and you will be sons and daughters of the Most High, for the Most High is kind to the ungrateful and the selfish. Be merciful, then, as your Father is merciful" (Luke 6:35–36). This is the Father Jesus' prayer is addressed to. This is the Father he stays in communion with. Divine love is revealed when we refuse to treat enemies the way they are treating us. Divine love is love, and it cannot be twisted by violence to respond violently. Jesus stays awake to the world of light as he enters the world of darkness.

Throughout his sufferings and dying Jesus is never a victim or a failure. The incidents on the way of the cross show him always in touch with divine love and always manifesting it. He tells the women of Jerusalem they need not weep for him (Luke 23:27–31). He may be dying, but he is still in touch with divine love. They should look to themselves. Although they are not physically on the road to the cross, their refusal to receive the love of God puts them on a path of destruction. He also refuses the temptation to come down from the cross and, implicitly, to avenge himself on his persecutors. In fact, he forgives those who crucify him (Luke 23:34). This power of forgiveness comes from his interior contact with God. Finally, he hands his spirit over to his Father at the hour of death (Luke 23:46). Although his spirit was never separated from his Father, death brings a complete surrender, a total offering. He is what he is, never anything less. In the way Jesus died divine love is shown to be more powerful than human violence.

This is the glory of the Messiah that can be entered into only through suffering. The glory of the Messiah is not related to military victories and triumphant parades and monumental feasts. It is his fidelity in extending the divine offer of love to a world resistant to salvation. His suffering and dying simultaneously reveal both this divine love and human violent refusal. However, these two players in the divine-human adventure are not equal. Resurrection is just one more creative unfolding of divine love. So given this God and given this world, "Was it not necessary that the Messiah suffer these things in order to enter into his glory?"

Jesus never stopped being the Son of God. He was the Son of God at the supper and the Son of God on the cross. In both places he was carrying out his mission, pouring life into life so other life could grow strong. Sometimes that life is received and sometimes that life is rejected. But the offer is never withdrawn. It ultimately comes from a reality so simple that it has only one style: self-giving.

The wager is that this unremitting flow of love will eventually entice human beings to give up their violent ways. The first letter of Peter (2:22–24) envisions the workings of this spiritual power: "He committed no sin, and no deceit was found in his mouth." He was never out of touch with divine love, never alienated by sin. The deeper communion with God flowed through him. Truth was all he spoke. "When he was abused, he did not return abuse. When he suffered, he did not threaten. But entrusted himself to the one who judges justly." He was not violently reactive. He did not enter into that temptation. He stayed connected to a more profound justice. "He himself bore our sins in his body on the cross." Our sins are all the actions motivated by our being alienated from the Divine Source. These actions — the ridicule, the rejection, the beatings, the nailing, the killing — are taken into his body, "so that free from sins, we might live for righteousness." Taken into his body means taken away from us. We are left without sin. Therefore, we are open to divine love.

The Son of God accomplished his mission, but not in a way that conventional wisdom can understand. People did not initially respond. Yet he responded to their lack of response in such a way that he made it possible for them to respond. He took away the block. Giving his body meant one thing at the supper and another thing at the cross, but in both places he gave what he had received. He saw what love had to do and he did it. "Whatever it takes" is the driving force of the single-hearted Christ. "By his wounds you have been healed."

Why did he suffer and die? The physical, social, and psychological meanings do not go far enough. The Lukan stories spiral us into the world of spirit. In this world the mystery of Jesus' suffering and dying is not solved. It is only deepened, and deepened in the direction of love, a love we "sometimes see, and then not."

A First Reflection: Finding a Love Larger Than Loss

I recently had the privilege to conduct some sessions of spiritual reflection with older Americans. The setting was a housing development, and the youngest of the group of eight was eighty-three and the oldest was ninety-two. Seven women and one man. Men are not long distance runners.

The background theory was that old age is a time of loss. There are physical, psychological, and social losses. The body is declining, aspects of the mind are not as sharp, and many relationships have been broken by sickness, death, and confinement. However, it may be a time of spiritual growth. It may be possible to develop spiritually even while there is decline in other areas of life. So it says here.

In one session I told stories of suffering. I thought it would be of interest since the room was a sea of suffering. Heart attacks, strokes, crippling arthritis, some mild dementia. Three of the women had cared for their husbands who suffered from Alzheimer's disease before it was a household word. Don't old people think about suffering all the time?

The first story was a Hindu tale about the passion to alleviate sufferings. It is a good story. But it did not get much of a response. Although everyone there was busy every day alleviating their suffering — pills, doctor visits, etc. — they did not pick up on the story.

The next story I told was a quick plot summary of the gospel of Mark followed by a word-by-word telling of the crucifixion scene. I stressed that God accompanies human suffering. We do not suffer alone. Since suffering has a tendency to isolate us, I thought the revelation of a divine presence in the midst of rejection and pain would be healing. Most of all I thought it would start people talking. Although everyone there was Christian and most were very religious, St. Mark and I bombed. Very little action.

The final story was a tale of a woman who lost her husband. She was inconsolable. The grief lasted so long she felt she would never love and live again. Finally, she goes to see a holy man. It is spiritual storytelling's oldest ploy: "Maybe the holy man will help." She enters his hut (why do holy men always live in huts?) and tells her tale. He says that he would like to help her but he is cold. Could she go around to the neighboring houses and gather some wood? They could make a fire, his old bones would be warmed, and then they could address her grief. She agrees, but as she is leaving he says to her, "Only take wood from a house that has lost no one."

Three women in the group said in unison. "She didn't get any wood."

I paused and finally said, "That's what the story says."

"But her grief lifted." This line, the actual last line of the story, came from a frail woman who earlier had asked us to pray for her husband. Recently, they had to be separated because his Alzheimer's had progressed to a point where he was uncontrollable.

Never at a loss for words, I said, "That's what the story says."

Then they talked. They all talked.

I sat back and listened.

I didn't listen *to* one thing or *for* one thing. I listened to it as a whole. It was many notes, but a single piece of music was being played. It came to me slowly. When I saw it, it was obvious.

Suffering wasn't a problem for them. It was just what is. It was not an offense to be railed against, an insult to who they were, or something they feared and fought every waking minute. It was just what was there. As someone once said, "It is not *my* pain. It is *the* pain."

Their real struggle was not with the unfairness of life or with their pain and loss. They may have wanted suffering and loss to stop, but they did not seriously toy with that fantasy. Their struggle was how to keep loving with diminished resources. They were concerned with loving "unto the end." Suffering was engaged from that point of view.

I believe that is also the point of view of the Lukan Christ. His life was played out in public, in social and political arenas. Most of our lives play in more private theaters. He did not want to lose love as he lost life. People were going to take his life from him. They would also try to take his love. They would succeed in snatching the first. They would fail in stealing the second. Resurrection witnesses to the durability of love.

These women and this man are losing life. Enemies are not

taking it from them. Time and finitude is wearing down their vitality. In the process they are trying not to lose love. In the story grief was so powerful it took love from the woman. She not only lost her husband, she lost her desire to love. Her path of healing was to join suffering humanity in its struggle not to be undone by what befalls it. Dostoevsky prayed to be worthy of his sufferings. I take that to mean he hoped to be able to find the resources of love within himself strong enough to shine through his diminishments.

When we read the dramatic events of Jesus' life, we look at him from a distance and admire. When we pause to discern what drives us and engage in an inner glance at the strivings of our Spirit-filled souls, he is close. "Stay with us." The disciples asked this because when he talked with them on the road they sensed a love that was larger than loss. Not for a millisecond did he hesitate. "And he went in and stayed with them."

A Second Reflection: Sacrifice as Zest for the Earth

I have often wondered about our giving, the endless secret acts of self-sacrifice, the countless pourings of life into life so that other life could grow strong. Are they just there and gone? Is time as good as its billing? Is it the great devourer of all things?

Self-giving probably dominates our days, but it is often missing from our conversations. We have to be reminded that it is a major part of our comings and goings. We are quick to reach for our trophies, name our triumphs, cite our awards. We forget the times we have reached out. That was something we did in between the important events. It was decent, but not noteworthy, and certainly not the secret essence of who we are. It is sentimental to watch George Bailey in *It's a Wonderful Life* be reminded of his good deeds as an antidote to suicide. However, that's a movie, a Christmas movie to boot.

What if we looked at breaking bread and breaking bodies as the primary human activity because it corresponds with divine activity? What if we were all a sacrifice into the world process?

This sacrificial impulse is an *original* component of life and *precedes* all those particular "aims" and "goals" which calculation, intelligence, and reflection impose upon it later. We have *the urge to sacrifice* before we ever know why, for what and for whom! Jesus' view of nature and life, which sometimes shines through his speeches and parables in fragmented and hidden allusions, shows quite clearly that he understood this fact.*

Who we are is there before we know it, and it is operating in a covert way throughout our ego-driven lives. We are an undercover agent to ourselves — a secret sacrificer masquerading as a megalomaniac.

My grandfather used to play a dawn-of-time game with me. I was small, maybe four or five. He would take a cookie or biscuit or roll in his hand and show it to me. He would put both hands behind his back and then bring them back in front. Both hands were closed into fists.

"If you can guess what hand the cookie is in, you can have it," he would say.

I would walk around his hands trying to catch a glimpse of cookie between the cracks of his fingers. But his hands were large and the cookie was well tucked inside. Finally, I would venture a guess and tap a hand. Both hands would open and turn over, flat as plates. On both hands was half a cookie. The scoundrel had broken the cookie in half behind his back.

I would say, "Pop, you cheated!"

But by that time he had eaten one of the halves. He would say to me, "You had better hurry."

I think we break bread and life like that — half for us and half for others. I think Jesus ate the bread he broke and fed himself on his own life. Sacrificers are fed by their own sacrifice. That is a secret we seldom see. There is more love when it is given away than when it is kept, more love for those who give it and more love for those who receive it. In the world of Spirit there is no scarcity.

---

*Max Scheler, *Ressentiment* (New York: Free Press of Glencoe, 1961), 89.

The mystery of self-giving is deeper still.

Teilhard de Chardin reflected quite deeply on this notion of self-giving.* He thought a true act was one in which we give something of our own life. Acts like these were undertaken with the intention of constructing a work of "abiding value." The greatest joy was cooperating as "one individual atom in the final establishment of a world." Personal immortality held little attraction for him. "It is enough for me that what is best in me should pass, there to remain forever, into one who is greater and finer than I." To contribute was more essential than to survive. Could it be: to contribute is to survive?

As you might imagine, Teilhard's friends told him they did not know what he was talking about. "Work, eat, drink, make love, and get on with it," they insisted. But Teilhard did not give up easily. He responded, "You are not searching to the full depth of your heart and mind. And that, moreover, is why the cosmic sense and faith in the world are dormant in you. You find satisfaction in the fight and the victory, and it is there that the attraction lies. But can you not see, then, that what is satisfied in you by effort is the passion for *being finally and permanently more?* ... Your zest for life is still emotional and weak."

There it is. That is what self-giving is about. It is zest for life and the cosmic sense that you are participating in the divine-human adventure of the world.

When?

When you break a cookie with your grandson.

And other times.

When you meet violence with the offer of love.

---

*Pierre Teilhard de Chardin, "How I Believe," in *Christianity and Evolution* (New York: Harcourt Brace Jovanovich, 1969), 109–15.

ALSO BY

JOHN SHEA

STARLIGHT
Beholding the Christmas Miracle All Year Long

"A wonderful book, which, like the Christmas season itself,
stirs the cold embers of the heart into fire."
— *Spiritual Book News*

"John Shea picks Christmas up carefully like a shining, decorative glass
Christmas-tree ball, then tosses it high in the air, calling out, 'Look!'
Yuletide magic suspends Christmas like a delicate glass ball, and while it
floats there, Shea points out its many sparkling features. And boy,
are you going to be glad.... What a great gift for giving!"
— *Praying Magazine*

"For those seeking a deeper meaning of Christmas than may be found
in shopping malls, or for anyone at a point of despair,
this is a rewarding book."
— *American Library Association Booklist*

0-8245-1272-3; $10.95

Please support your local bookstore, or call 1-800-395-0690.
For a free catalog, please write us at
THE CROSSROAD PUBLISHING COMPANY
370 LEXINGTON AVENUE, NEW YORK, NY 10017

We hope you enjoyed Gospel Light. *Thank you for reading it.*

crossroad